Top Chemistry Grades for You

Lawrie Ryan

GCSE Revision Guide for AQA

Nelson Thornes

a Wolters Kluwer business

Contents

Introduction

Revision Technique

Exam Technique

Revision Cards (detachable, for revision in spare moments)

To see the latest Exam Specification for AQA Science, visit **www.aqa.org.uk**

To see this Exam Specification 'mapped' with the relevant pages in *Chemistry for You*, visit **www.chemistryforyou.co.uk**

Introduction

Top Chemistry Grades for You is designed to help you achieve the best possible grades in your GCSE examination.

It focusses on exactly what you need to do to succeed in the AQA Science examinations, whether for Core Science, for Additional Science, or for the full GCSE Chemistry qualification, at both Foundation Tier and Higher Tier.

It includes a section on 'How Science works', which is an important part of all the AQA Science examinations.

This revision book is best used together with the *Chemistry for You* textbook, but it can also be used by itself.

There are also books for
Top Biology Grades for You and
Top Physics Grades for You.

For each section in the AQA GCSE Science examination specification, there is a Topic as shown on the opposite page.

For each Topic there are 2 double-page spreads:

- a **Revision** spread, which shows you exactly what you need to know (see below), and

- a **Questions** spread, which lets you try out Homework questions and some real Exam questions on this topic.
  The answers to these are given at the back of the book.

In addition, for a section of Topics there is:

- a **Sample Answer** spread, showing you answers at Grade-A level and at Grade-C level, with Examiners' Comments and Tips. These will help you to focus on how to improve, to move up to a higher grade.

Each Revision spread is laid out clearly, using boxes:

Each spread starts with some 'ThinkAbout' questions, to help you focus on the topic. The answers are shown at the bottom of the page.

Topic number and AQA reference

The pages show essential content for the exam.

Items are often boxed for clarity.

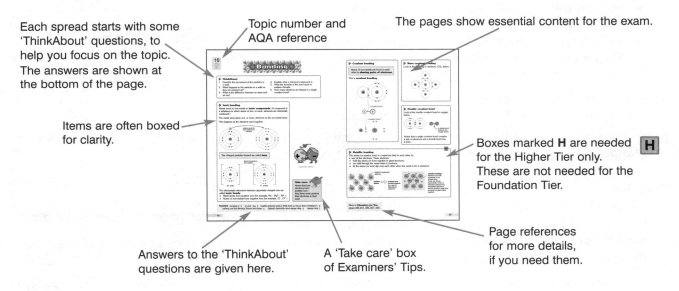

Boxes marked **H** are needed for the Higher Tier only. These are not needed for the Foundation Tier.

Answers to the 'ThinkAbout' questions are given here.

A 'Take care' box of Examiners' Tips.

Page references for more details, if you need them.

As a first step, go through this book and:

- If you are **not** studying for the Higher Tier, cross out all the boxes labelled **H**

- If you are **not** studying for the full GCSE Chemistry, cross out all of Topics 18 to 23.

On the front and back covers of this book there are detachable **Revision Cards**, with very brief summaries.

You can cut these out and use them to top up your revision in spare moments – for example, when sitting on a bus or waiting for a lesson.

Good luck in your exams!

Lawrie Ryan

Revision Technique

Prepare

1. Go through the book, crossing out any boxes that you don't need (as described at the bottom of page 3).

2. While doing this, you can decide which are your strong topics, and which are topics that you need to spend more time on.

3. You need to balance your time between:
   - **Revising** what you need to know about Chemistry.
     To do this, use the first double-page spread in each topic.
   - **Practising** by doing exam questions.
     To do this, use the second spread in each topic.
   Do these two things for each topic in turn.

Revise

4. Think about your best ways of revising. Some of the best ways are to do something *active*. To use active learning you can:
   - Write down **notes**, as a summary of the topic (while reading through the double-page spread).
     Use highlighter pens to colour key words.
   - Make a **poster** to summarise each topic (and perhaps pin it up on your bedroom wall).
     Make it colourful, and use images/sketches if you can.
   - Make a spider-diagram or **mind map** of each topic.
     See the example here, but use your own style:
   - Ask someone (family or friend) to **test** you on the topic.
   - **Teach** the topic to someone (family or friend).
   Which method works best for you?

5. It is usually best to work in a quiet room, for about 25–30 minutes at a time, and then take a 5–10 minute break.

6. It is often helpful to draw up a **Revision Calendar**, to keep a note of your progress:

Topic 4 AQA 1a.3
✓ 3rd April

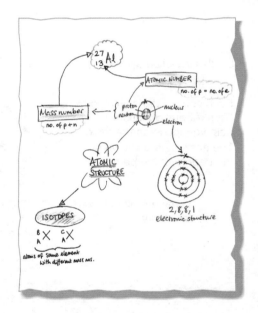

A **Mind Map** for Topic 9: Atomic Structure.

A Mind Map always makes more sense when you make it *yourself*.

Use colour and images if you can.

Practise

7. When you have revised a topic, and think you know it well, then it's important to practise it, by answering some **exam questions**. Turn to the second spread of the topic and answer the questions as well as you can.

8. When you have finished them, turn to the **Examination answers** that start on page 108.
   Check your answers. Can you see how to improve your answers in future?

9. If you have a **Revision Calendar** keep a record of your progress on it.

Topic 4 AQA 1a.3
✓ 3rd April
✓ 4th April

Re-revise and Top-up

10. It is important to re-revise each topic again, after an interval. The best intervals are after 10 minutes, after 1 day, and after 1 week (see the graphs in **Chemistry for You**, pages 384–385).

    For this top-up you can use the topic spread, your notes, poster or mind map, and the **Revision Cards** on the cover of this book.

A revision flowchart:

Choose a topic to revise.

1. Revise

- **Think About**: try the questions in the ThinkAbout box.
  The answers are at the bottom of the page.

- **Read** the rest of the double-page spread.
  Focus on any parts you are not sure about.

- **Do** make Notes, or a Poster, or a Mind Map.
  Highlight key points in colour.

- **Re-read** the spread after a break of 5–10 minutes.

- **Take care**: read the 'Take care' box.
  Can you see how you can use this advice?

2. Practise

- **Try** the questions on the double-page of questions.
  These are in the same style as the ones in the exam.

- **Check** your answers. The answers begin on page 108.
  Go back over anything you find difficult.

Then later:

Re-visit
Re-visit each topic 1 day later, and then 1 week later.
Read the double-page spread, your notes or Mind Map,
and the questions you answered.

Up your Grade
At the end of each section of topics, read the Sample
Answers at Grade A and Grade C.
Look at the Hints and Tips for improving your grade.

Top-up
Use the Revision Cards to remind you of the key points,
and test yourself.
Even better, make your own Revision Cards.

Examination Technique

Before the exam

1. Make sure you know the dates and times of all your exams, so that you are not late!
    See the table at the bottom of this page.

2. Make sure you know which topics are going to be examined on which paper.

3. On the night before the exam, it may help to do some quick revision – but don't do too much.
    Make sure you get a good night's sleep.

On the day of the exam

1. Aim to arrive early at the exam room.

2. Make sure that you are properly equipped with pens and pencils (including spares), a rubber, a ruler, a calculator (check the battery!) and a watch.

During the exam

1. Don't waste time when you get the paper. Write your name and candidate number (unless they are already printed).
    Read the instructions on the front page of the booklet, carefully, and make sure you follow them.

2. Read each question very carefully.
    In each question there is always a 'command' word that tells you what to do.
    If the question says '*State ...*' or '*List ...*' or '*Name ...*' then you should give a short answer.
    If the question says '*Explain ...*' or '*Describe ...*' or '*Why does ...*' or '*Suggest ...*' then you should make sure you give a longer answer.

    Put a ring round each 'command' word.

    Then <u>underline</u> the key words in the question.
    For example:

    (Describe) in detail what you would <u>see</u> when a small piece of <u>sodium</u> is placed in a trough of cold <u>water</u>.

    Then you can see exactly what is given to you in the question, and what you have to do.

    Make sure that you answer only the question shown on the exam paper (not the one that you wish had been asked).

One way of collecting information about all your exams (in all your subjects):

Date, <u>time</u> and room	<u>Subject,</u> paper number and tier	Length (time)	Types of question: – structured? – single word answers? – longer answers? – essays?	Sections?	Details of choice (if any)	Approximate time per mark (minutes)
5th June 9.30 Hall	Science Paper 1 (Chemistry) Higher Tier	90 mins	Structured questions (with single-word answers and longer answers)	1	no choice	1 min.

6

Answering the questions

Structured questions

- Make sure you know *exactly* what the question is asking.

- Look for the number of marks awarded for each part of the question. For example *(2 marks)* means that the Examiner will expect 2 main (and different) points in your answer.

- The number of lines of space is also a guide to how much you are expected to write.

- Make sure that you use any data provided in the question.

- Pace yourself with a watch so that you don't run out of time. You should aim to use about 1 minute for each mark. So if a question has 3 marks it should take you about 3 minutes.

- In calculations, show all the steps in your working. This way you may get marks for the way you tackle the problem, even if your final answer is wrong. Make sure that you put the correct units on the answer.

- Try to write something for each part of every question.

- Follow the instructions given in the question. If it asks for one answer, give only one answer.

- If you have spare time at the end, use it wisely.

Extended questions

- Some questions require longer answers, where you will need to write two or more full sentences.

- The questions may include the words '*Describe*...' or '*Explain*...' or '*Evaluate*...' or '*Suggest*...' or '*Why does*...'.

- Make sure that the sentences are in good English and are linked to each other.

- Make sure you use scientific words in your answer.

- As before, the marks and the number of lines will give you a guide of how much to write. Make sure you include enough detail with at least as many points as there are marks.

- For the highest grades you need to include full details, in scientific language, written in good English, and with the sentences linking together in the correct sequence.

For multiple-choice questions:
- Read the instructions carefully.
- Mark the answer sheet exactly as you are instructed.
- If you have to rub out an answer, make sure that you rub it out well, so no pencil mark is left.
- Even if the answer looks obvious, look at all the alternatives before making a decision.
- If you are not sure of the answer, then first delete any answers that look wrong.
- If you still don't know the answer, then make an educated guess!
- Ensure that you give an answer to every question.

How Science works

> **ThinkAbout:**

1. What do we call the things we see happen in our practical work?
2. What do we call it when we say what we think will happen in an investigation?

3. What do we call the things we learn from our investigations?
4. What do we call our comments on how to improve our investigation?

> **Collecting evidence**

Good scientists make sure their data provide evidence that is **reliable** and **valid**. Reliable evidence will be trustworthy. If you, or someone else, collected the data again it should be the same (or similar). You can trust reliable data. It is then valid evidence only if it also actually measures what you intended to find out about.

> **Making measurements**

You should also consider the **sensitivity** of your measuring instrument ie. the smallest change it can detect.

Accuracy tells us how near the true value your measurement is.

The **precision** of a measurement is also important. This is related to its smallest scale division on your measuring instrument.

> **Different types of variable**

We can classify variables into the following types:

- **Categoric** variables: These are variables that we can describe using words.
  Examples are 'type of acid' eg. hydrochloric acid, or 'type of carbonate' eg. calcium carbonate.
- **Ordered** variables: These are a type of categoric variable that we can put into an order.
  An example is 'surface area' of calcium carbonate, if you use 'large lumps / medium lumps / small lumps' as a way of describing the values of the variable.
- **Discrete** variables: These are variables that can only have whole number values.
  An example is 'the number of marble chips'.
- **Continuous** variables: These are variables that we can describe by any number, as their values are measurements eg. 17.5 cm^3.
  Examples are 'temperature' or 'mass'.

> **Presenting your data – tables**

As you carry out an investigation, you can record your data in a results table.

Scientists usually arrange their tables so that the **independent variable** (the one you change deliberately, step-by-step) goes in the first column.

The **dependent variable** (used to judge the effect of varying the independent variable) goes in the second column. For example, if you were investigating the effect of temperature on the time to collect a set volume of gas given off in a reaction, the table would have these headings:

Independent variable: **Temperature (°C)**	*Dependent variable:* **Time to collect 20 cm³ of gas (s)**

▷ Control variables

These are the variables we try to keep **constant** to make sure our tests are as fair as possible.
This is difficult in field studies and tests on living things. Sample sizes and control groups are important parts of collecting valid data in these investigations.

▷ Presenting your data – graphs

Then you can show the relationship (link) between the two variables by drawing a graph.
- The independent variable goes along the horizontal axis.
- The dependent variable goes up the vertical axis.

The graph you draw depends on the type of independent variable you investigated.
- If it is a continuous variable – you can display your results on a line-graph.
- If it is a categoric variable – you have to display your results on a bar chart.

▷ Relationships between variables

Once you have your graph to refer to, you can see what the relationship is between the two variables.

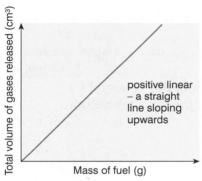

A positive linear (straight-line) relationship – slopes upwards. If the line starts at the origin (0,0) we call this a directly proportional relationship.
Other relationships are shown by curves. (See page 67.)

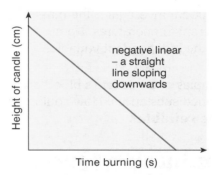

A negative linear relationship – slopes downwards

▷ Science and society

Other factors besides evidence can influence decisions that affect society.
You should consider whether:
- data presented is unbiased, eg. do scientists have a vested interest;
- political pressure is at work;
- the scientist is experienced and has a good reputation, or not;
- certain groups of people will benefit from having the work accepted.

▷ Evaluating your investigation

You should consider the reliability and validity of the measurements you make.
You can also improve reliability and validity by:
- looking up data from secondary sources, eg. on the Internet;
- checking your results by using an alternative method;
- seeing if other people following your method get the same results, ie. are your results reproducible?

▷ Limitations of Science

There are some questions that Science really helps us to answer. These are usually questions that start 'How can we …?'

But there are other questions based on beliefs and opinions that it can't answer. Society as a whole, which includes scientists, has to try to answer the 'Should we …?' type questions.

More details in *Chemistry for You*, pages 6–17.

Answers: 1. observations 2. prediction 3. conclusion 4. evaluation

How Science works

Homework Questions

1 What type of variable can:
(a) be described using words,
(b) be a type of categoric variable that can be put into an order,
(c) be described by any number,
(d) only have whole number values? *(4 marks)*

2 Some copper is weighed on a sensitive balance. The data it produces is very **accurate**. What can you say about this data compared to the actual mass of the copper? *(1 mark)*

3 A student repeats an experiment several times. The teacher tells the student that the set of results is very **reliable** and **precise**. What does the teacher's comment suggest about the results? *(1 mark)*

4 A student attempts to measure the pH of a cola drink using universal indicator solution. Why might the result *not* be **valid**? *(1 mark)*

5 A student investigates the mass of copper sulfate that will dissolve in water heated to different temperatures. Name:
(a) the independent variable,   (b) the dependent variable,   (c) **one** control variable. *(3 marks)*

6 Samples of an athlete's blood are sent to three different laboratories to be tested for banned substances. How could you tell if the methods used by the three laboratories were **reliable**? *(1 mark)*

_____
11
marks

Examination Question

An experiment was performed to study the amount of oxygen in air.
Some iron wool was put in a measuring cylinder.
This was placed in a beaker of water as shown in diagram A.
After a few days the water level rose in the measuring cylinder as shown in diagram B. The iron slowly formed rust which is iron oxide.

(a) Explain why the level of water in the cylinder rose.

....

.... *(2 marks)*

(b) The experiment was repeated several times. The volume of air used up was measured each time. The results are given in the table:

Experiment	1	2	3	4
Volume of air used up in cm³	20	18	22	19

(i) Calculate the average volume of air used up.

....

.... *(1 mark)*

(ii) Suggest why the volume of air used up was not the same for all the experiments.

....

.... *(1 mark)*

(iii) Suggest why the experiment was repeated.

.... *(1 mark)*

_____
5
marks

Multiple Choice Examination Questions

1 Match words **A**, **B**, **C** and **D** with the spaces **1–4** in the sentences.

A a categoric

B an ordered

C a discrete

D a continuous

A student did four investigations to study the rate of reaction between marble chips and dilute acid.

The first investigated the effect of using small, medium and large marble chips. The size of the marble chips is ...**1**... variable.

The second investigated the effect of varying the temperature. Temperature is ...**2**... variable.

The third investigated the effect of using different acids. The type of acid used is ...**3**... variable.

The fourth investigated the effect of using different whole numbers of marble chips. The number of marble chips is ...**4**... variable.

2 Which graph shows that the variables are directly proportional to each other?

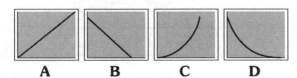

A   B   C   D

3 Which electronic balance would probably be the most expensive?
A balance which weighs to the nearest:

A 0.01 g

B 1 g

C 0.0001 g

D 0.1 g

4 Which question **cannot** be answered by doing experiments?

A Is the temperature of the Earth rising?

B Should we burn less fossil fuel?

C How much carbon dioxide is in the air?

D Is limestone decomposed by heat?

5 Which thermometer is the most sensitive and will produce the most precise data?

	Temperature range over which it will measure in °C	Smallest division on thermometer scale in °C
A	−10 to 110	1
B	0 to 500	2
C	−5 to 50	0.1
D	0 to 100	0.2

6 Experimental evidence that is both reliable **and** answers the original question is said to be:

A accurate

B fair

C precise

D valid

7 A student designed an experiment to compare the viscosity (thickness) of water and sunflower oil. The time taken for 200 cm^3 of the liquid to flow through a small hole was measured. The experiment was repeated for each liquid.

Liquid	Time taken for the liquid to flow through the hole in seconds				
	1	2	3	4	Average
water	76	79	75	80	77.5
oil	125	126	123	119	

(a) The average time taken for oil was:

A 122.5 s

B 124.0 s

C 123.3 s

D 126.0 s

(b) The dependent variable was:

A the size of the hole

B the temperature of the liquid

C the type of liquid

D the time taken to flow through the hole

(c) The independent variable was:

A the size of the hole

B the temperature of the liquid

C the type of liquid

D the time taken to flow through the hole

Answers on page 108

ESSENTIAL CHEMISTRY

▶ **ThinkAbout:**

1. Name the metals with the following chemical symbols:
   a) Zn   b) Li   c) Fe   d) Cr

2. Give the chemical symbols for the following metals:
   a) sodium   b) potassium   c) copper

▶ **Atoms and elements**

An element is a substance that cannot be broken down chemically into simpler substances. That's because:

> **Elements contain only one type of atom.**

There are about 100 different elements. These are listed in the Periodic Table. (See below.)

Each atom has a small, dense nucleus surrounded by electrons. (See opposite.)

▶ **Chemical symbols**

Each type of atom has its own chemical symbol. Look at the table below:

Element	Symbol	Element	Symbol
Hydrogen	H	Neon	Ne
Carbon	C	Iron	Fe

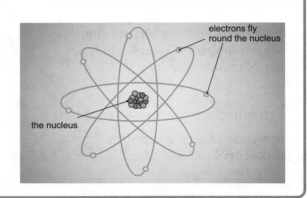

electrons fly round the nucleus

the nucleus

▶ **The Periodic Table**   *Each colour shows a chemical family of similar elements.*

Group numbers 1	2										3	4	5	6	7	0
							H 1 hydrogen									He 2 helium
Li 3 lithium	Be 4 beryllium										B 5 boron	C 6 carbon	N 7 nitrogen	O 8 oxygen	F 9 fluorine	Ne 10 neon
Na 11 sodium	Mg 12 magnesium										Al 13 aluminium	Si 14 silicon	P 15 phosphorus	S 16 sulphur	Cl 17 chlorine	Ar 18 argon
K 19 potassium	Ca 20 calcium	Sc 21 scandium	Ti 22 titanium	V 23 vanadium	Cr 24 chromium	Mn 25 manganese	Fe 26 iron	Co 27 cobalt	Ni 28 nickel	Cu 29 copper	Zn 30 zinc	Ga 31 gallium	Ge 32 germanium	As 33 arsenic	Se 34 selenium	Br 35 bromine	Kr 36 krypton
Rb 37 rubidium	Sr 38 strontium	Y 39 yttrium	Zr 40 zirconium	Nb 41 niobium	Mo 42 molybdenum	Tc 43 technetium	Ru 44 ruthenium	Rh 45 rhodium	Pd 46 palladium	Ag 47 silver	Cd 48 cadmium	In 49 indium	Sn 50 tin	Sb 51 antimony	Te 52 tellurium	I 53 iodine	Xe 54 xenon
Cs 55 caesium	Ba 56 barium	La 57 lanthanum	Hf 72 hafnium	Ta 73 tantalum	W 74 tungsten	Re 75 rhenium	Os 76 osmium	Ir 77 iridium	Pt 78 platinum	Au 79 gold	Hg 80 mercury	Tl 81 thallium	Pb 82 lead	Bi 83 bismuth	Po 84 polonium	At 85 astatine	Rn 86 radon

Look at the Periodic Table above:
Similar elements are lined up in columns called **groups**.

Answers: 1. a) zinc b) lithium c) iron d) chromium   2. a) Na b) K c) Cu

▷ Atoms bonding together

Atoms bond to each other by transferring or sharing electrons. If the atoms are of different elements we get a compound formed.

> **A compound contains atoms of two or more elements bonded together.**

Transferring electrons

Sharing electrons

▷ Conservation of mass

We can classify changes as physical changes or chemical changes:

- **Physical changes** do not produce any new substances, and are often easy to reverse. Changes of state, such as melting or boiling, are examples of physical changes.

- However, in **chemical changes** (or reactions) new substances are made. There are energy changes that accompany chemical changes. Burning carbon is an example of a chemical change.

We can represent these chemical reactions by **word equations**:

> **reactants ⟶ products**

For example:

carbon + oxygen ⟶ carbon dioxide

The law of **conservation of mass** states that:

> **the total mass of the reactants equals the total mass of the products.**

▷ Chemical formula

The formula of a compound tells us the **ratio** of the different types of atoms bonded together.
For example, sulfur dioxide, SO_2, contains twice as many oxygen atoms as sulfur atoms.

▷ Balanced equations

Chemical reactions can also be shown by **balanced equations** made up of chemical formulae. These must have the same numbers of each type of atom on either side of the equation. For example:

$$2H_2 + O_2 \longrightarrow 2H_2O$$

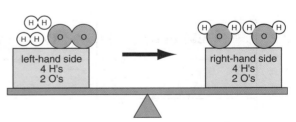

left-hand side
4 H's
2 O's

right-hand side
4 H's
2 O's

Make sure you can see why this equation is balanced:

$$2NaNO_3 \longrightarrow 2NaNO_2 + O_2$$

More in *Chemistry for You*, pages 20–27, 30, 40.

Essential chemistry

Homework Questions

1   What do we mean by the term chemical 'element'? *(1 mark)*

2   What do all elements have in common? *(1 mark)*

3   Find the symbols for these elements:
aluminium   sulfur   bromine   helium   nickel *(5 marks)*

4   What do these symbols stand for?
H   Mg   C   Cl   Ca *(5 marks)*

5   Most elements have simple symbols, but a few elements have rather odd symbols, such as:
Sn (Stannum) is the symbol for tin,   Au (Aurum) is the symbol for gold
Pb (Plumbum) is the symbol for lead   Ag (Argentum) is the symbol for silver
Why do some elements have strange symbols? *(1 mark)*

6   Which elements make up Group 2 of the periodic table? *(5 marks)*

7   Explain the differences between 'an element' and 'a compound'. *(2 marks)*

8   What information can you get from a substance with the formula H_2SO_4? *(1 mark)*

9   Explain in your own words the difference between a physical change and a chemical change, and give **one** example of each kind of change. *(3 marks)*

10 Is this equation balanced? $Mg + O_2 \longrightarrow MgO$
Explain your answer. *(1 mark)*

25 marks

Examination Question

(a) Here are some common substances:

pure water   milk   salt   sand   copper   aluminium

Put each substance in to the correct column:

Element	Compound	Mixture

(6 marks)

(b) Which of the above substances has the chemical name 'sodium chloride'?

....

(1 mark)

7 marks

Multiple Choice Examination Questions

1 Ca is the chemical symbol for:

   A carbon

   B calcium

   C caesium

   D cadmium

2 The minimum number of atoms in a chemical compound is:

   A 1

   B 2

   C 3

   D 4

3 Compounds are formed when atoms of different elements:

   A break up

   B dissolve in water

   C are mixed together

   D bond together

4 Which of the following is a chemical change?

   A melting ice

   B boiling water

   C boiling an egg

   D melting chocolate

5 Compounds are harder to separate into their components than mixtures because:

   A compounds are always solids

   B mixtures are always liquids

   C compounds have chemical bonds between the components

   D mixtures have chemical bonds between the components

6 The particles which orbit the nucleus of an atom are called:

   A electrons

   B protons

   C positrons

   D neutrons

7 When atoms join together to make compounds they transfer, or share,

   A a nucleus

   B one, or more, protons

   C one, or more, electrons

   D one, or more neutrons

Read the following carefully, then choose answers to fill in the gaps from the words below:

'In a chemical change a ...**8**... substance is always made. There is always a ...**9**... change in a chemical reaction. ...**10**... petrol is an example of a chemical change.

8 **A** unknown

   B new

   C chemical

   D similar

9 **A** physical

   B state

   C temperature

   D colour

10 A Evaporating

   B Pouring

   C Freezing

   D Burning

Answers on page 108

BUILDING MATERIALS FROM Rocks

ThinkAbout:

1. Name three rocks that are made mainly from calcium carbonate.
2. What do we call the reaction between an acid and an alkali?

3. a) Which gas is given off when calcium carbonate reacts with acid?
   b) How would you test for this gas?

▶ Limestone

Limestone is made up mainly of **calcium carbonate** ($CaCO_3$).
It is used as a building material itself, but is also used to make **cement**. Powdered limestone is heated in a rotating kiln with clay (or shale) to make the cement.

Cement is the basis of **concrete** – the most widely used building material. This is made by mixing cement, sand and crushed rock, together with water. The mixture sets in a slow chemical reaction to form a very hard, rock-like substance.

▶ The lime kiln

When we heat limestone in a lime kiln it makes quicklime (calcium oxide, CaO):

$$CaCO_3(s) \xrightarrow{heat} CaO(s) + CO_2(g)$$

The reaction is called **thermal decomposition**.

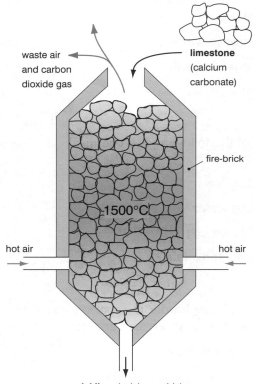

waste air and carbon dioxide gas

limestone (calcium carbonate)

fire-brick

1500°C

hot air   hot air

quicklime (calcium oxide)

▶ Decomposing other carbonates

Like calcium carbonate, other metal carbonates also undergo thermal decomposition. The reactions are similar. For example:

zinc carbonate $\xrightarrow{heat}$ zinc oxide + carbon dioxide

$$ZnCO_3(s) \longrightarrow ZnO(s) + CO_2(g)$$

carbonate being tested

limewater

heat

By adding water to quicklime, we get slaked lime (calcium hydroxide, $Ca(OH)_2$) which is a cheap alkali. This, or powdered limestone, can be used to raise the pH of acidic soil.

Powdered limestone is also used to neutralise lakes affected by acid rain.

Answers: 1. limestone, chalk, marble   2. neutralisation   3. a) carbon dioxide   b) limewater turns milky

▶ Glass

We make glass by heating sand, limestone and soda (sodium carbonate).

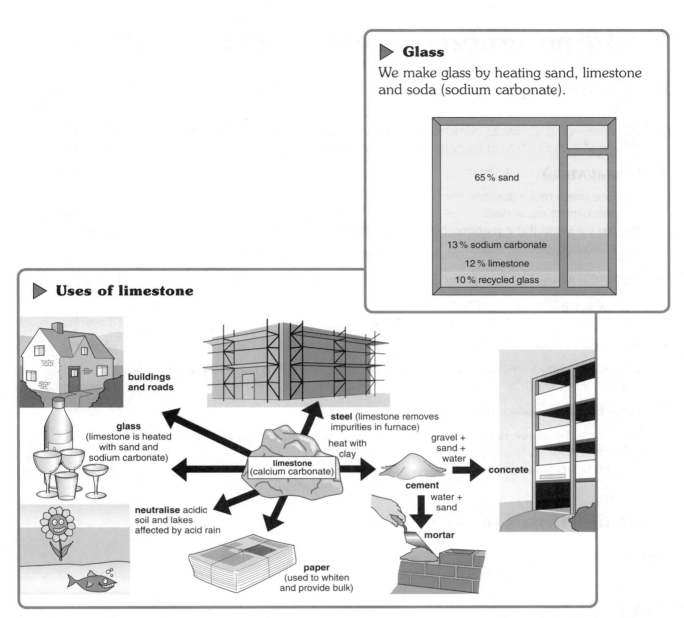

65 % sand

13 % sodium carbonate

12 % limestone

10 % recycled glass

▶ Uses of limestone

buildings and roads

glass
(limestone is heated with sand and sodium carbonate)

steel (limestone removes impurities in furnace)

heat with clay

gravel + sand + water

concrete

limestone
(calcium carbonate)

cement

water + sand

neutralise acidic soil and lakes affected by acid rain

mortar

paper
(used to whiten and provide bulk)

▶ Reactions of limestone

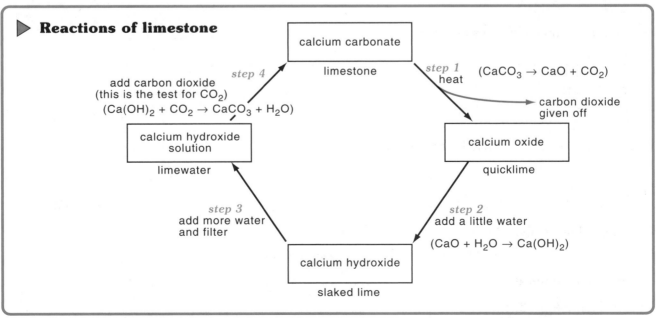

calcium carbonate

limestone

step 1
heat $(CaCO_3 \rightarrow CaO + CO_2)$

carbon dioxide given off

step 4
add carbon dioxide
(this is the test for CO_2)
$(Ca(OH)_2 + CO_2 \rightarrow CaCO_3 + H_2O)$

calcium hydroxide solution

limewater

calcium oxide

quicklime

step 3
add more water and filter

step 2
add a little water

$(CaO + H_2O \rightarrow Ca(OH)_2)$

calcium hydroxide

slaked lime

More in *Chemistry for You*, pages 109–118.

Building materials from rocks

Homework Questions

1 (a) What is the chemical name for the main compound found in limestone? *(1 mark)*
(b) What is the chemical formula of this compound? *(1 mark)*

2 What is concrete made from? *(4 marks)*

3 (a) Complete this equation:
calcium oxide + water ⟶ .... *(1 mark)*
(b) Now rewrite the equation above using chemical symbols. *(3 marks)*

4 Explain in your own words what we mean by 'thermal decomposition'. *(1 mark)*

5 Name the two substances formed when we heat copper carbonate. *(2 marks)*

6 Write the equation for question 5
(a) in words, and (b) in chemical symbols. *(2 marks)*

7 What makes up about 65% of the glass-making mixture? *(1 mark)*

8 Why is powdered limestone sometimes deliberately added to lakes in countries like Norway and Sweden? *(1 mark)*

9 What has to be added to cement to make mortar? *(2 marks)*

10 What would you see happening when you blow into a colourless solution of calcium hydroxide?
Explain your answer. *(2 marks)*

21 marks

Examination Question

(a) Name the three elements in chalk.

1. ....

2. ....

3. .... *(3 marks)*

(b) Explain why chalk is called a compound.

....

.... *(2 marks)*

(c) When chalk is heated it forms a new solid and a gas:

calcium carbonate ⟶ calcium oxide + a gas

(i) Name a reactant. ....

(ii) Name a product. ....

(iii) What type of reaction is shown? ....

(iv) What gas is made in the reaction? .... *(4 marks)*

9 marks

Multiple Choice Examination Questions

1 Which one of these is *not* made up mainly of calcium carbonate?

   A limestone

   B marble

   C gypsum

   D chalk

2 Which one of these is *not* made from limestone?

   A bricks

   B mortar

   C cement

   D concrete

3 The products made when calcium carbonate is heated strongly are:

   A calcium oxide and carbon dioxide

   B calcium oxide and carbon monoxide

   C calcium carbonate and carbon dioxide

   D calcium carbonate and carbon monoxide

4 The common name for the chemical calcium oxide is:

   A lime dust

   B quicklime

   C limestone

   D powdered limestone

5 The pH number for a solution of calcium hydroxide could be:

   A 3

   B 5

   C 7

   D 9

6 Which of the following is a thermal decomposition reaction?

   A $CaCO_3 + 2HCl \longrightarrow CaCl_2 + H_2O + CO_2$

   B $CaCO_3 \longrightarrow CaO + CO_2$

   C $CaO + H_2O \longrightarrow Ca(OH)_2$

   D $Ca(OH)_2 + CO_2 \longrightarrow CaCO_3 + H_2O$

7 Which of the following is *not* used to make glass?

   A sand

   B sodium carbonate

   C limestone

   D sodium hydroxide

8 In industry, limestone undergoes thermal decomposition in:

   A a cracker

   B a cooling tower

   C a kiln

   D a fractionating column

9 Which is the correct equation?

   A $ZnCO_3 \longrightarrow Zn + CO_3$

   B $ZnCO_3 \longrightarrow ZnO_2 + CO$

   C $ZnCO_2 \longrightarrow Zn + CO_2$

   D $ZnCO_3 \longrightarrow ZnO + CO_2$

10 The chemical test for carbon dioxide gas is:

   A a piece of moist red litmus paper turns blue

   B a flame test gives a red colour

   C a lighted wood splint pops

   D a solution of limewater turns milky/cloudy

Answers on page 108

Useful products from METAL ORES

▶ ThinkAbout:

1. Name a metal that is less reactive than copper.
2. Which metal is used to make cooking foil?
3. Which metal is used to make electrical wires?
4. Why are iron gates usually painted?
5. What do we call it when a compound is broken down by electricity?

▶ Carbon in the Reactivity Series

A few metals are found in the Earth's crust as metals themselves (for example, gold). Most are found as metal compounds.

> **Ores** are rocks that contain enough metal to make it economical to extract the metal.

We can predict how to extract a metal from its position in the Reactivity Series.

The highly reactive metals are difficult to extract. We use electrolysis to extract these metals, such as sodium or aluminium.

The metals of medium reactivity can be extracted by **reduction** of the oxides with carbon.

potassium
sodium
magnesium
aluminium
CARBON
zinc
iron
tin
lead
copper

carbon cannot be used to extract the more reactive metals

these metals can be extracted using carbon

$$2\,PbO \;+\; C \;\rightarrow\; CO_2 \;+\; 2\,Pb$$

carbon is oxidised
lead oxide is reduced

REDUCTION is the LOSS of OXYGEN   −O

OXIDATION is the ADDITION of OXYGEN   +O

Reduction and oxidation are chemical opposites

▶ The blast furnace

We extract iron in a giant **blast furnace**.

The iron from a blast furnace goes on to make **steel** (which usually contains about 96% iron). This impure iron is too brittle to have many uses. But removing all the impurities makes iron too soft. (See diagram on next page – the layers of identical iron atoms can slide over each other too easily.)

We have to protect the iron in steel from rusting. For example, we can also add some nickel and/or chromium in the steel-making process to form **stainless steel** (used in cutlery). Stainless steel is an example of an **alloy**. (See next page.)

Low carbon steels are easy to shape (good for car bodies).
High carbon steels are hard (good for drilling and cutting).

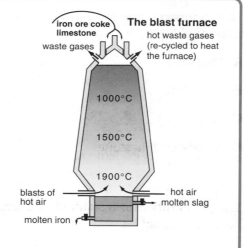

iron ore coke limestone

The blast furnace

waste gases

hot waste gases (re-cycled to heat the furnace)

1000°C

1500°C

1900°C

blasts of hot air

hot air
molten slag

molten iron

▶ Alloys

Alloys are mixtures of metals, designed to improve their properties. The layers of atoms in an alloy do not slip over each other as easily as in a pure metal. This makes them harder.

The latest alloys developed, called **smart alloys**, can return to their original shape if they get deformed. They seem to 'remember' their original shape when heated to a certain temperature.

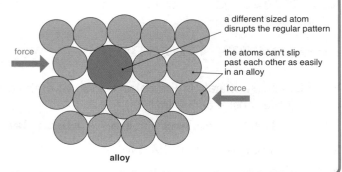

force

a different sized atom disrupts the regular pattern

the atoms can't slip past each other as easily in an alloy

force

alloy

▶ Titanium and aluminium

Alloys of titanium and aluminium are both expensive. That's because aluminium is extracted by electrolysis – which requires a lot of energy. Titanium is extracted in a multi-stage process (which involves reduction using a reactive metal that has been extracted itself by electrolysis). Despite the cost, both metals are used because they resist corrosion, eg. titanium in hip joints. Aluminium alloys are used to make aeroplanes because of their low density.

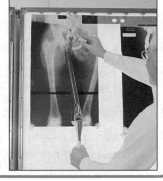

This hip joint is made from an alloy of titanium

▶ The transition metals

In the central block of the Periodic Table we find the **transition metals**.
These have the typical properties of metals.
They usually:

- have high melting points
- are good conductors of heat
- are good conductors of electricity
- can be hammered into shapes (are malleable)
- can be drawn out into wires (are ductile).

Transition metals are tough and hard

Transition metals are strong

Sc	Ti	V	Cr	Mn	Fe	Co	Ni	Cu	Zn
									Ag
			W				Pt	Au	

▶ Copper

Copper is a useful transition metal.
Although it is not reactive, we use electrolysis to purify the metal. The copper extracted from its ores is too impure to use in electrical wiring.

Copper ores that contain lots of copper are getting harder to find. So new methods to extract the metal are being developed. For example, low-grade ores can yield their copper by using bacteria.

This is called **bio-leaching**.

Yum – cop a load of this delicious rock!

More in *Chemistry for You*, pages 72–81, 95–98, 270–273.

Useful products from metal ores

Homework Questions

1 Place these metals in the correct order of their chemical reactivity.
(Put the most reactive first.)

      lead   copper   tin   aluminium   zinc   sodium *(6 marks)*

2 Why is potassium very hard to extract from its compounds? *(1 mark)*

3 Explain why we say that lead oxide has been reduced in this reaction:
$$2PbO + C \longrightarrow CO_2 + 2Pb$$
                                                            (1 mark)

4 Name the **four** raw materials that are used in a blast furnace. *(4 marks)*

5 Why do we add nickel and chromium to molten iron, when making steel? *(1 mark)*

6 (a) Name six transition metals. *(6 marks)*
    (b) List six properties of transition metals. *(6 marks)*

7 Copper can be extracted by electrolysis. Explain what we mean by 'electrolysis'. *(1 mark)*

8 (a) What is meant by the term 'alloy'? *(1 mark)*
    (b) Give the names of two common alloys. *(2 marks)*
    (c) Suggest one use for a 'smart' alloy which can remember its shape
        if it is deformed. *(1 mark)*

9 What properties of titanium make it suitable for use in a replacement hip joint? *(1 mark)*

10 What properties of aluminium make it suitable for use in making aeroplane bodies? *(1 mark)*

11 What properties of copper make it suitable for use in our 1p and 2p coins? *(1 mark)*

12 Carbon is not a metal, yet it is often included in tables of metal reactivities.
Suggest why this might be. *(1 mark)*

                                    34 marks

Examination Question

The diagram shows the arrangement of atoms in an **alloy**.

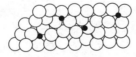

Key
○ Iron atoms
• Carbon atoms

(a) What is meant by an **alloy**?

....

.... *(2 marks)*

(b) Name the alloy represented in the diagram.

.... *(1 mark)*

(c) Give **one** advantage of using this alloy instead of pure iron.

....

.... *(1 mark)*

(d) Which elements are used to make brass?

.... *(1 mark)*

           5 marks

Multiple Choice Examination Questions

1   An example of a metal found by itself in the Earth's crust is:

   A magnesium

   B zinc

   C iron

   D gold

2   Which is the correct order of reactivity for these metals (from most reactive to least reactive)?

   A potassium, zinc, tin, copper

   B zinc, potassium, tin, copper

   C tin, copper, zinc, potassium

   D potassium, tin, zinc, copper

3   Which metal is extracted by electrolysis?

   A gold

   B silver

   C aluminium

   D tin

4   A metal which can be extracted by heating its ore with carbon is:

   A sodium

   B lead

   C magnesium

   D aluminium

5   High carbon steel is most likely to be used for:

   A car bodies

   B conducting electricity

   C making a drill bit

   D reinforcing concrete

6   Which of these is *not* a typical property of transition metals?
Transition metals:

   A are malleable

   B are ductile

   C are hard

   D have low melting points

7   Copper is used to make electrical wiring because:

   A it is a very good electrical conductor

   B it is a very good thermal conductor

   C it does not react with acids

   D it is a very cheap metal

8   Metals can be mixed to make alloys. The main purpose of alloying is:

   A to improve the appearance of the product

   B to make the product stronger

   C to increase the melting point of the product

   D to improve the colour of the product

9   Electrolysis is a technique used to

   A extract iron from iron(III) oxide

   B pass electricity through molten copper

   C make metals join together in an alloy

   D extract reactive metals from their ores

10 Which of these is a possible equation?

   A $C + Al_2O_3 \longrightarrow 2Al + CO_3$

   B $C + 2PbO \longrightarrow 2Pb + CO_2$

   C $C + Na_2CO_3 \longrightarrow 2Na + C_2O_3$

   D $C + 2CaCO_3 \longrightarrow 2Ca + 3CO_2$

Answers on page 109

USEFUL PRODUCTS FROM

▶ ThinkAbout:

1. Finish this sentence:
   Crude oil is a …
   A mixture of elements
   B mixture of compounds
   C pure compound
   D pure element.
2. What is a hydrocarbon?

3. Crude oil is a fossil fuel. Name two others.
4. Finish this sentence:
   We find crude oil beneath layers of s… rock.
5. Why didn't the animals and plants that formed fossil fuels just rot away when they died?

▶ Crude oil

Most of the compounds in crude oil are called **hydrocarbons**. They contain only hydrogen and carbon atoms.

Crude oil contains a **mixture of hydrocarbons**.

(A mixture consists of two or more elements or compounds that are *not* chemically combined. The substances in the mixture still have their original properties. This allows them to be separated.)

The hydrocarbons in crude oil all have different boiling points. They can be separated into compounds with similar boiling points by **fractional distillation**.

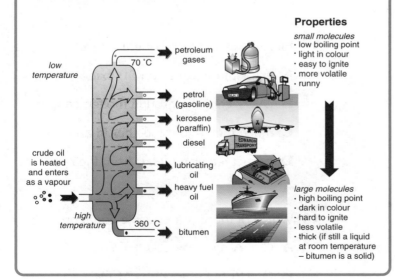

Properties

small molecules
· low boiling point
· light in colour
· easy to ignite
· more volatile
· runny

large molecules
· high boiling point
· dark in colour
· hard to ignite
· less volatile
· thick (if still a liquid at room temperature – bitumen is a solid)

▶ Alkanes

Many of the hydrocarbons in crude oil are called **alkanes**.

Their molecules contain only single bonds.
They are known as **saturated** hydrocarbons.

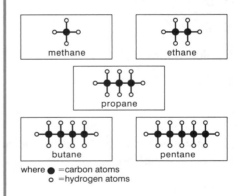

methane   ethane   propane   butane   pentane

where ● =carbon atoms
      ○ =hydrogen atoms

The general formula of the alkanes is:

$$C_n H_{2n+2}$$

More in *Chemistry for You*, pages 139–152.

▷ Combustion of hydrocarbons

Hydrocarbons from the fractional distillation of crude oil are very important fuels.
Look at the experiment below:

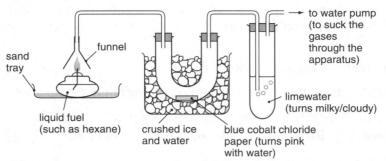

In plenty of oxygen, we get complete combustion:

> **hydrocarbon + oxygen ⟶ carbon dioxide + water**

▷ Pollution from fuels

Carbon dioxide from burning fossil fuels contributes towards **global warming**. Look at the graph opposite:

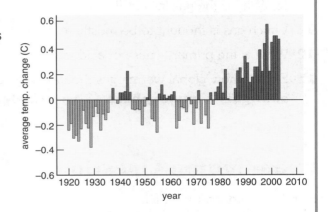

Fossil fuels can contain sulfur compounds as impurities. When these burn we get sulfur dioxide given off. This causes **acid rain**.

Inside engines we do not get complete combustion of hydrocarbons. There is a limited amount of oxygen. We get **incomplete combustion**. Some of the carbon in the fuel is turned into **carbon monoxide**. This toxic gas stops your blood carrying oxygen around your body.

Incomplete combustion also gives off **tiny solid particles** of carbon and unburnt hydrocarbons. These can cause breathing problems and may cause cancer.
People are also worried that these specks of pollution will cause **global dimming**. The particles absorb the Sun's energy before it reaches the Earth's surface.

▷ Fighting pollution

There is not much we can do about carbon dioxide given off from fossil fuels – except use less energy. Sulfur can be removed from fuels before we burn them. Acidic sulfur dioxide from power stations can be removed from gases released by reacting the gases with a basic substance.

*Nitrogen oxides (which contribute to acid rain) are changed into harmless nitrogen gas by **catalytic converters** in car exhausts. These also change carbon monoxide into carbon dioxide.*

Useful products from oil

Homework Questions

1 Sue wanted to separate water from salt solution, so she used a simple distillation.
Pete knows that this method would not work to separate the components of crude oil.
Why not? *(1 mark)*

2 What do we mean by the term 'hydrocarbon'? *(1 mark)*

3 Why can the components of crude oil be separated by fractional distillation? *(1 mark)*

4 Put these oil fractions in increasing order of their boiling points:
   diesel   petrol   bitumen   kerosene   fuel oil *(5 marks)*

5 Why are the alkanes called *saturated* hydrocarbons? *(1 mark)*

6 What is the formula for the alkane which contains 8 carbon atoms? *(1 mark)*

7 What is the chemical formula for pentane? *(1 mark)*

8 (a) What two products are formed in the complete combustion of butane, C_4H_{10}? *(2 marks)*
   (b) What toxic gas could be formed by the **in**complete combustion of butane? *(1 mark)*
   (c) Why is the gas in part (b) toxic? *(1 mark)*

9 Which gas is thought to be mostly responsible for global warming? *(1 mark)*

10 What is the primary cause of acid rain? *(1 mark)*

11 Explain how global warming is thought to be caused – using these words in your answer:
   sunlight   atmosphere   re-radiates   radiation   absorbed *(5 marks)*

22 marks

Examination Question

Petrol is a hydrocarbon fuel.

(a) Complete this sentence.
   Hydrocarbons are compounds which are made from the elements

   .... and .... only. *(2 marks)*

(b) This apparatus was used to study the combustion of a hydrocarbon fuel.

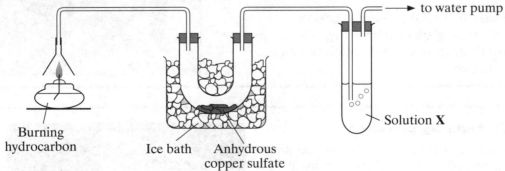

to water pump

Burning hydrocarbon

Ice bath   Anhydrous copper sulfate

Solution **X**

(i) Name the substance which changed the anhydrous copper sulfate from white to blue.

   .... *(1 mark)*

(ii) Carbon dioxide is also produced when the hydrocarbon fuel is burned.
   Name the solution, labelled **X** on the diagram, which tests for carbon dioxide.

   .... *(1 mark)*

4 marks

Multiple Choice Examination Questions

1 Which of the following is *not* a hydrocarbon?

   A CH_4

   B C_3H_8

   C C_4H_{10}

   D $C_6H_{12}O_6$

2 Which of these oil fractions has the lightest colour?

   A petrol

   B kerosene (paraffin)

   C diesel

   D lubricating oil

3 Which of these oil fractions would produce the most soot when it burns?

   A petrol

   B kerosene (paraffin)

   C diesel

   D lubricating oil

4 Which of these compounds is *not* an alkane?

   A C_4H_{10}

   B C_3H_8

   C C_6H_{14}

   D C_2H_4

5 Hexane is an alkane with six carbon atoms. Its formula is:

   A C_6H_6

   B C_6H_{12}

   C C_6H_{14}

   D C_6H_{22}

6 Which hydrocarbon among the following is most volatile?

   A propane (C_3H_8)

   B butane (C_4H_{10})

   C octane (C_8H_{18})

   D decane ($C_{10}H_{22}$)

7 What are the missing parts from this equation?
$$C_2H_4 + 3O_2 \longrightarrow \text{..............} + \text{..............}$$

   A $CO_2 + H_2O$

   B $CO + H_2$

   C $2CO_2 + 2H_2O$

   D $2CO_2 + H_2O$

Read the following carefully, then choose answers to fill in the gaps from the words below:

'When a fuel has insufficient ...**8**... to burn properly, ...**9**... is produced. This gas is ...**10**... to humans as it reduces the amount of oxygen in the bloodstream.

8   **A** energy

     B carbon atoms

     C oxygen

     D chemical bonds

9   **A** heat energy

     B water vapour

     C carbon dioxide

     D carbon monoxide

10 **A** useful

     B necessary

     C vital

     D poisonous

Answers on page 109

Getting the Grades – Iron and Steel

Try this question, then compare your answer with the two examples opposite ▶

Bridges are often made from steel.

(a) Explain, in terms of atoms, why pure iron would be too soft for making bridges.

....

....

....

.... *(2 marks)*

(b) The steel used for bridges is an alloy made from iron with a small amount of carbon. Explain, in terms of atoms, how the addition of a small amount of carbon makes the steel suitable for bridges.

....

....

.... *(2 marks)*

(c) The strength of a metal can be tested by measuring the force needed to snap a wire made from the metal. An apparatus that could be used is shown in the diagram. Great care must be taken, since, when the wire snaps, the end of the wire could hit somebody.

The apparatus is used to compare the strength of two different metals.

Suggest two variables that must be controlled to make the experiment a fair test.

1. ....

2. .... *(2 marks)*

(d) Read the information about recycling of steel and then answer the questions.

> Scrap steel reduces related water pollution, air pollution, and mining wastes by about 70%. It takes four times as much energy to make steel from virgin ore.
>
> Recycling steel and tin cans saves 74% of the energy used to produce them from raw materials. At least 70–80% of the tin on a can is saved when you recycle it. This cuts down mining waste and preserves a valuable ore source.
>
> Every time a ton of steel is recycled, 2500 pounds of iron ore, 1000 pounds of coal and 40 pounds of limestone are preserved.
>
> The recycling process involves simply melting the scrap steel and then removing impurities.

(i) Explain why mining iron ore causes environmental problems.

....

.... *(3 marks)*

(ii) Explain why as much steel as possible should be recycled.

....

.... *(3 marks)*

12 marks

(a) The atoms in iron are arranged in layers. ✓
    These layers can slide over each other which
    makes the metal soft. ✓
(b) The carbon atoms are not the same size as
    the iron atoms. ✓ They cause the layers of
    atoms to be distorted so that they do not
    slide over each other as easily. ✓
(c) 1. length of the wire ✓
    2. diameter of the wire ✓
(d) (i) Mining scars the landscape ✓ and destroys
        the habitats of plants and animals. ✓
    (ii) Much less energy is needed to recycle
         steel than to make it from iron ore. ✓
         Recycling also means that valuable ores
         are conserved. ✓

Each of these parts is worth three marks. This means that three ideas are required in each case. The candidate has only given two ideas in each part.

10 marks = Grade A answer

Improve your Grades   A up to A*

▶ Part (c) is testing some of the knowledge and understanding of 'How Science works' which is part of the AQA Specification. Remember to revise this work before any examinations. This candidate needed to make another point in each part of (d), e.g. in (i) the production of large amounts of dust could be given as an example of the 'air pollution' mentioned in the question, and in (ii) some reduction of a pollution effect could be noted such as the release of less CO_2 – a greenhouse gas.

GRADE 'C' ANSWER

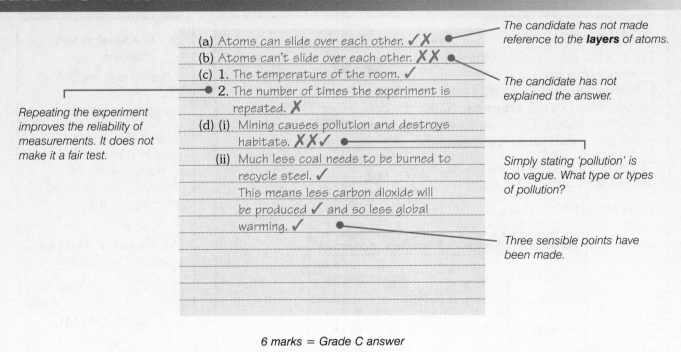

(a) Atoms can slide over each other. ✓✗
(b) Atoms can't slide over each other. ✗✗
(c) 1. The temperature of the room. ✓
    2. The number of times the experiment is
       repeated. ✗
(d) (i) Mining causes pollution and destroys
        habitats. ✗✗✓
    (ii) Much less coal needs to be burned to
         recycle steel. ✓
         This means less carbon dioxide will
         be produced ✓ and so less global
         warming. ✓

*The candidate has not made reference to the **layers** of atoms.*

The candidate has not explained the answer.

Repeating the experiment improves the reliability of measurements. It does not make it a fair test.

Simply stating 'pollution' is too vague. What type or types of pollution?

Three sensible points have been made.

6 marks = Grade C answer

Improve your Grades   C up to B

▶ Questions will be set in which you are required to read a passage and then answer some questions. Do read the passage very carefully as some of the answers will be in the information given.

Polymers & ethanol from OIL

ThinkAbout:

1. What do we mean by 'thermal decomposition'?
2. Why do we use catalysts in industry?
3. What is the advantage of biodegradable plastics?
4. How many bonds can a) a carbon atom, and b) a hydrogen atom form?

▶ Cracking

Most of the fractions from crude oil are used as fuels.
Fuels such as petrol are in great demand.

So some large hydrocarbon molecules in the heavier fractions are **'cracked'** into smaller, more useful molecules to use as fuels.
For example:

decane $\longrightarrow$ octane + ethene
$C_{10}H_{22} \longrightarrow C_8H_{18} + C_2H_4$

The large molecules are heated and passed over a catalyst to break them down.
Cracking is an example of a **thermal decomposition** reaction.

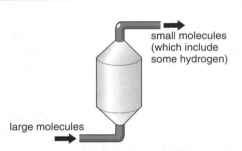

A cracker in an oil refinery

It's a cracker

▶ Alkenes

Look at the picture of an ethene molecule opposite:
Ethene belongs to a 'family' of hydrocarbons called **alkenes**. Notice the double bond between the carbon atoms. Compounds with one or more double bonds are called **unsaturated** compounds.

double bond — *an ethene molecule*

The general formula of the alkenes with one double bond is: C_nH_{2n}

Look at the table below:

Name	Formula	Structure of molecule
ethene	C_2H_4	H—C=C—H (with H's)
propene	C_3H_6	H—C=C—C—H (with H's)

▶ Ethanol from ethene

Ethanol is a useful fuel and solvent that we can make from ethene.

In industry, we react ethene gas with steam in the presence of a catalyst (concentrated phosphoric acid):

C_2H_4 (g) + H_2O (g)
ethene   steam

catalyst

C_2H_5OH (g)
ethanol

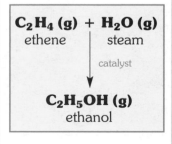

Answers: 1. the breakdown of a substance by heat 2. to speed up reactions 3. they rot away when we dispose of them 4. a) 4 bonds b) 1 bond

30

Which method to make ethanol?

Ethanol can be made as shown on the previous page. However, this uses up supplies of crude oil. It can also be made by fermenting sugar, which we get from plants eg. sugar cane. The plants are a renewable source of energy. Ethanol made by either method gives off carbon dioxide (a greenhouse gas) when it burns. However, the plants take in CO_2 as they grow. Therefore ethanol from **fermentation** helps to tackle global warming.

Polymers

During cracking, we also get small reactive molecules, such as ethene, formed.
These can react with each other when heated under pressure.

In the presence of a catalyst, these molecules join together to make large molecules used to make plastics.

> The small molecules are called **monomers**.
> The very large molecule they form is called a **polymer**.
> The reaction is called **addition polymerisation**.

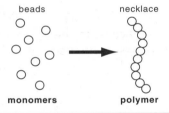

beads → necklace
monomers → polymer

Making different polymers

We can make different polymers by:
- starting with different monomers – Look at the examples below:

Monomer		Polymer
ethene	⟶	poly(ethene)
styrene	⟶	poly(styrene)
vinyl chloride	⟶	poly(vinyl chloride)

- using different conditions – Ethene reacts to make poly(ethene). But we can make poly(ethene) with different properties by varying the conditions of the reaction, eg. the temperature, pressure or catalyst used.
High density poly(ethene) is much stronger with a high melting point than low density poly(ethene).
Poly(ethenol) forms slimy polymers with a variety of 'gooeyness' (viscosity) by adding different amounts of borax.

Some uses of plastics

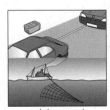

poly(ethene)
(made from ethene)

poly(propene)
(made from propene)

New developments in polymers
- New packaging materials
- waterproof coatings for fabrics
- dental polymers
- wound dressings
- hydrogels
- shape memory polymers (which can respond to changes in their surroundings).

Getting rid of plastics

One of the advantages of many plastic objects is their 'long life'. They are resistant to attack by other substances. However, this becomes a disadvantage when we have finished with them. They take up valuable space in land-fill sites.

That's why chemists are developing degradable plastics. These are broken down in nature by bacteria (biodegradable) or by light.

More in *Chemistry for You*, pages 153–163, 166–168.

Polymers and ethanol from oil

Homework Questions

1 Which oil fraction has the largest worldwide demand? *(1 mark)*

2 When crude oil has been through the fractional distillation process, some of it is further refined by cracking. Why is this? *(1 mark)*

3 Explain the difference in molecular structure between ethane C_2H_6 and ethene C_2H_4. *(1 mark)*

4 What is the formula for the alkene with four carbon atoms and a double bond between two of these carbon atoms? *(1 mark)*

5 Ethene C_2H_4, is much more reactive than ethane C_2H_6. Why is this? *(1 mark)*

6 Name the substance made when steam reacts with ethene, in the presence of a catalyst. *(1 mark)*

7 What is the name of the polymer formed when lots of ethene molecules join together? *(1 mark)*

8 This is the chemical formula of a substance commonly used to make a polymer:

$$\begin{array}{ccc} H & & H \\ | & & | \\ C & = & C \\ | & & | \\ H & & Cl \end{array}$$

    (a) What is the name of this monomer? *(1 mark)*

    (b) What is the name of the polymer made from this monomer? *(1 mark)*

9 Name the common polymer made from this monomer: C_3H_6 *(1 mark)*

10 Suggest a suitable use for high-density poly(ethene). *(1 mark)*

11 Have you ever heard the term 'intelligent packaging'? If you have access to the Internet, find out what intelligent packaging is all about – and suggest some uses for this new technique. *(2 marks)*

_____
13
marks

Examination Question

Two reactions of ethene are shown.

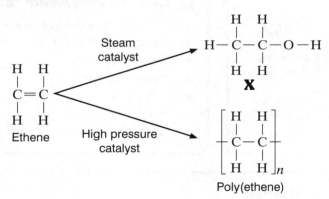

(a) Name substance **X**.

.... *(1 mark)*

(b) Write the symbol equation for the reaction shown above that is used to make **X**.

.... *(1 mark)*

(c) **X** can be used as a fuel. Why would **X** made by the method above be described as 'a fuel made from a **non-renewable** source'?

_____
3
marks

.... *(1 mark)*

Multiple Choice Examination Questions

1 Match the words in **A**, **B**, **C** and **D** with the numbers **1–4** in the sentences below:

  A thermal decomposition

  B cracked

  C monomers

  D polymers

When large molecules are broken down into smaller ones, the large molecules are said to be …**1**…

This type of reaction is an example of …**2**…

Lots of the small molecules or …**3**… produced go on to be joined together to make very large molecules. The very large molecules which are formed are known as …**4**…

2 The molecule of ethene has:

	Number of carbon atoms	Number of hydrogen atoms	Number of double bonds
A	2	2	1
B	2	4	1
C	4	4	2
D	2	4	2

3 The alkene which has 8 carbon atoms and has a double bond between two of its carbon atoms, has the formula:

  A C_8H_8

  B C_8H_{12}

  C C_8H_{16}

  D C_8H_{18}

4 The molecule which has 2 carbon atoms, 6 hydrogen atoms and 1 oxygen atom is called:

  A methanol

  B ethanol

  C propanol

  D butanol

5 Teflon is:

  A a non-stick plastic coating used for frying pans, etc.

  B used for making milk crates

  C made into new style plastic guttering

  D used to make plastic covered chairs for students to use in schools

6 Plastics that can be broken down by bacteria once thrown away are said to be:

  A smart

  B thermoplastics

  C thermosetting plastics

  D biodegradable

7 Most plastic objects are:

  A cheap, made from oil, and are difficult to make

  B cheap, made from coal, and are easy to make

  C cheap, made from oil, and are easy to make

  D expensive, made from oil, and are easy to make

Answers on page 110

Plant oils

▷ ThinkAbout:

1. Which of these processes is involved in distillation?
   freezing, evaporation, condensation, melting
2. Which gas causes acid rain?
3. What word describes two liquids that don't mix?
4. How can we separate a mixture of coloured substances?

▷ Extracting the oil from plants

In order to get the oil from a plant, we have to break open its cells to release it.
There are two main ways to break down the cell walls:

- pressing (applying pressure),
- distillation (heating with steam).

▷ Emulsions

Plant oils do not dissolve in water. We say that oil and water are **immiscible**.

Oil and water form two separate layers. The oil is less dense than the water so it floats on top.

When you shake the salad dressing, you get tiny blobs of oil spread (dispersed) throughout the watery vinegar. We call this type of mixture an **emulsion**.

▷ Emulsifiers

An **emulsifier** stops oil and water separating out into layers.

The molecules of an emulsifier have a long chain made of carbon and hydrogen atoms. This part of the molecule dissolves well in oil. At one end of the molecule it has a charged part that dissolves well in water. Look at a model of an emulsifier molecule below:

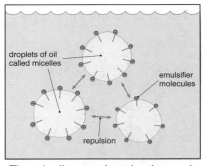

The micelles repel each other and remain dispersed in the emulsion

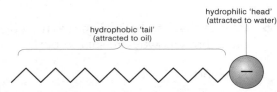

So an oil droplet becomes 'studded' with emulsifier molecules. The droplets are called **micelles**.

Look at the diagram opposite:
Because the surface of each micelle carries the same charge, they repel each other. This keeps the droplets of oil spread throughout the water, as an emulsion.

Lots of foods have artificial emulsifiers added. They make liquids thicker, and improve the texture and appearance of food.

▷ Food additives

As well as emulsifiers, processed foods can contain other additives.
These can:

- improve appearance (colourings),
- improve taste (flavour enhancers),
- extend shelf-life of the foods (preservatives / antioxidants).

Once the additives have been tested and approved they are given an **E number**. You can see these listed on food packaging.

Food scientists can identify additives using chemical analysis. They can separate and identify food colourings using **chromatography**. Look at the chromatogram opposite:

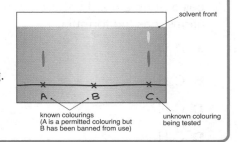

Answers: 1. evaporation and condensation 2. sulfur dioxide 3. immiscible 4. chromatography

▷ Margarines

Margarines are made from plant oils. Sunflower oil is a popular choice for margarine manufacturers.

Margarines are often advertised as being 'high in poly-unsaturates'. This means that the hydrocarbon chain in the oil molecules contains lots of double bonds between carbon atoms. Others are 'mono-unsaturated'. As the name suggests, they have one double bond per hydrocarbon chain.

Testing for C=C bonds

Shake up some margarine with a little ethanol to dissolve it. Then add some bromine water.

> An **unsaturated** compound decolourises bromine water. Unsaturated compounds also react with iodine.

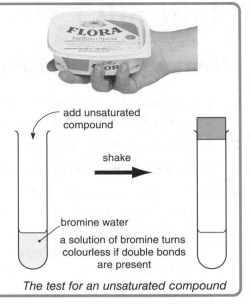

add unsaturated compound

shake

bromine water

a solution of bromine turns colourless if double bonds are present

The test for an unsaturated compound

▷ Making margarine

The problem with making margarine is that the plant oils are liquids at room temperature. So they are too runny to spread on bread. They are less viscous than saturated oils or fats, such as butter. Saturated molecules have straighter chains that can pack together better. They have stronger forces between their molecules.

However, the oils can have their melting points raised and be made thicker. We can react them with hydrogen gas to saturate some of the double bonds. The process is called **hardening**.

The reaction takes place at about *60°C with a nickel catalyst*.

$$\text{plant oil} + \text{hydrogen} \xrightarrow[60°C]{\text{nickel}} \text{margarine (less unsaturated than the oil)}$$

As the molecules straighten, the oils get more viscous. Chemists have to add just the right amount of hydrogen. If they add too much, the margarine will be too hard to spread when it comes out of the fridge; too little, and the margarine will be too runny if left out of the fridge.

The soft, solid margarine is easier to make cakes and pastry with, as well as spreading smoothly on bread.

More in *Chemistry for You*, pages 174–186.

▷ Biodiesel

We use oilseed rape to make **biodiesel**. Sunflower oil is also used. Even recycled vegetable oil from chip shops can be used as the starting material for biodiesel!

Advantages of biodiesel

- Our supplies of fossil fuels are running out. So getting fuel from a source that can be regrown every year will help.
- Pollution is also reduced by burning biodiesel. It still gives out carbon dioxide, a greenhouse gas, just like diesel. However, the plants used to make it absorb carbon dioxide as they grow.
- It does not produce sulfur dioxide so reduces acid rain. The particulates that diesel engines give out, which can cause cancer, are also reduced.
- Biodiesel is biodegradable. So it breaks down if spilt in water.

Disadvantages of biodiesel

- Large areas of farmland are used to produce fuel instead of food. This could pose problems if we start to rely on it.
- People are also worried about the destruction of habitats of endangered species. Large areas of tropical forest where they live are being turned into palm plantations for the palm oil.
- Biodiesel can start to freeze at low temperatures, turning to sludge. It can also oxidise and start to form polymers, which can gum up engines.

Plant oils

Homework Questions

1 If you have oily hands (say from cleaning a bicycle chain) and you place your hands into some hot water, your hands will not come clean. Why not? *(1 mark)*

2 Explain the meaning of the word 'immiscible'. *(1 mark)*

3 What is the difference between a solution and an emulsion? *(1 mark)*

4 Look up the word 'hydrophilic' in a dictionary. Write down its meaning, and suggest a meaning for the word 'hydrophobic'. *(2 marks)*

5 Look at the ingredients in a bottle of mayonnaise and find the name of the emulsifier, which is being used. (You could also use a search engine on the Internet to look up 'mayonnaise'!) *(1 mark)*

6 Look at the ingredients of several processed foods in your kitchen. List any additives used as food colours. *(2 marks)*

7 Recently food colours called 'Sudan 1' and 'Sudan 3' have caused problems for the food industry. What sort of problems did they cause? *(1 mark)*

8 Some time ago, there was a margarine advert on TV, which told everyone how good that product was because it had a high 'poly-unsaturate' content.
What is a 'poly-unsaturate'? *(1 mark)*

9 Explain the essential differences between 'oils' and 'fats'. *(2 marks)*

10 (a) What is biodiesel? *(1 mark)*
   (b) Suggest one reason why scientists are trying to develop 'biodiesel' for us to use. *(1 mark)*

14
marks

Examination Question

(a) Here are some descriptions of some types of chemicals:
   A A substance, which speeds up a chemical reaction, but is not used up itself in the reaction.
   B A liquid made from oilseed rape or sunflower oil.
   C A long molecule with both hydrophilic and hydrophobic parts.
   D A vegetable oil with lots of carbon–carbon double bonds.

   Which description best matches the description of:

   (i) Biodiesel?   ....

   (ii) A substance used to make margarine?   ....

   (iii) A catalyst?   ....

   (iv) An emulsifier?   ....   *(4 marks)*

(b) Bromine water is often used to test for the presence of a compound containing one or more double bonds.
   Explain how bromine water is used, and the outcome of the test for an unsaturated compound.

   ....

   ....

   (2 marks)

6
marks

Multiple Choice Examination Questions

1 A technique which may be used to extract oils from plant cells is called

   A thermal decomposition

   B steam distillation

   C fractional distillation

   D simple distillation

2 When a mixture of oil and water is stirred it will later separate into two layers. This is because:

   A the oil is more dense than the water

   B the water and oil are immiscible

   C the water is less dense than the oil

   D it may not have been stirred properly

3 Emulsifiers are used in the food industry to:

   A improve the taste of the product

   B make liquids 'thinner'

   C improve the texture of the food

   D make the food keep fresh for a longer time

4 A technique which may be used to separate and identify food colourings is:

   A steam distillation

   B thermal decomposition

   C evaporation

   D chromatography

5 Which is a correct equation?

   A $C_2H_4 + Br \longrightarrow C_2H_4Br$

   B $C_2H_6 + Br_2 \longrightarrow C_2H_6Br_2$

   C $C_2H_4 + Br_2 \longrightarrow C_2H_4Br_2$

   D $C_2H_4 + Br_2 \longrightarrow C_2Br_2 + 2H_2$

6 When making margarine, a nickel catalyst is used in order to:

   A reduce the operating temperature of the reaction

   B make the vegetable oils easier to use

   C react with the vegetable oils

   D speed up the reaction

7 Vegetable oils provide us with a large amount of:

   A nutrients and energy

   B protein

   C starch

   D sugars

8 Fats have higher melting points than vegetable oils because:

   A they have reacted with the catalyst

   B they have been hydrogenated

   C their molecular structure has broken down

   D they contain food additives

9 Which of these is not normally an emulsion?

   A butter

   B mayonnaise

   C motor car engine oil

   D ice cream

10 A solution of bromine can be used to test whether or not a substance is unsaturated. We can also use a solution of:

   A iodine

   B limewater

   C sodium hydroxide

   D ethanol

Answers on page 110

Earth and its Atmosphere

Atmosphere

▶ **ThinkAbout:**

1. Complete these examples of metamorphic rock:

   m _ _ _ _ _   s _ _ _ _

2. Complete these examples of igneous rock:

   g _ _ _ _ _ _   b _ _ _ _ _

3. Name the main noble gas found in the air.
4. Why are people worried about increasing levels of carbon dioxide in the atmosphere?

▶ **Structure of the Earth**

The Earth is made up from:

- a thin outer crust
- a mantle (under the crust stretching almost half-way to the centre of the Earth)
- a core (the outer core is liquid; the inner core is solid; both parts are made from iron and nickel).

The Earth's crust and uppermost part of its mantle (called the **lithosphere**) is split up into **tectonic plates**. These move very slowly on convection currents set up in the mantle. The heat comes from radioactive rocks.

We can work out the plate boundaries by looking at where we get earthquakes and/or volcanoes. Even with modern technology, scientists cannot predict accurately when an earthquake or volcanic eruption will take place.

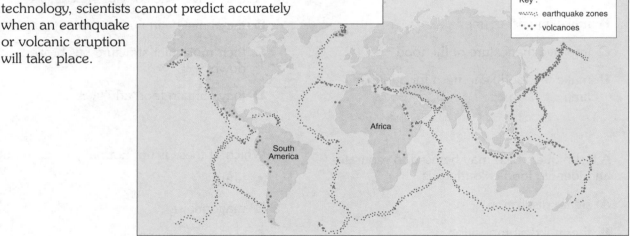

Key:
····· earthquake zones
····· volcanoes

Africa

South America

▶ **Changing theories**

A German scientist, Alfred Wegener, put forward his theory of continental drift in 1915. He saw how the shapes of Africa and South America matched, as did their rocks and fossils. He suggested the two land masses were once joined and must have slowly drifted apart. However, scientists already had a theory to explain the Earth's features. They thought its surface wrinkled as the Earth cooled down and formed mountains.

Eventually Wegener's ideas were accepted about 50 years after his death when scientists found evidence of tectonic plates moving beneath the oceans.

Answers: 1. marble, slate 2. granite, basalt 3. argon 4. global warming/greenhouse effect

▶ The atmosphere

The air is made up of about:
- 80% nitrogen gas
- 20% oxygen gas
- small amounts of other gases, including carbon dioxide, water vapour and noble gases.

History of the atmosphere

In the Earth's first billion years, its early atmosphere came from volcanoes.

It was probably mainly **carbon dioxide** (like Mars and Venus now). There was no oxygen. This only arrived once the first plants had evolved.

During photosynthesis, the plants took in carbon dioxide and gave out oxygen.

Most carbon became 'trapped' in fossil fuels and carbonate rocks.

The oceans were formed when water vapour from the volcanoes fell as rain as the Earth cooled down. The small amount of ammonia and methane in the early atmosphere was removed when they reacted with oxygen gas.

The history of our atmosphere

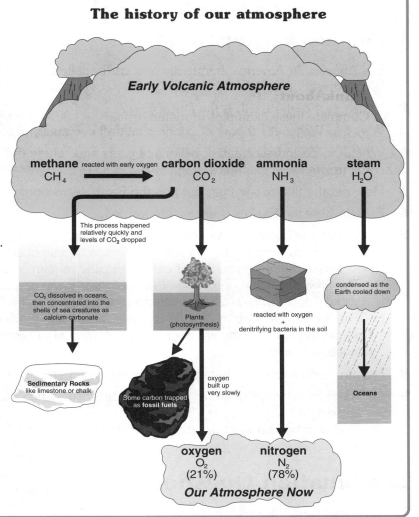

Early Volcanic Atmosphere

methane CH_4 — reacted with early oxygen → carbon dioxide CO_2 — ammonia NH_3 — steam H_2O

This process happened relatively quickly and levels of CO_2 dropped

CO_2 dissolved in oceans, then concentrated into the shells of sea creatures as calcium carbonate

Plants (photosynthesis)

reacted with oxygen + denitrifying bacteria in the soil

condensed as the Earth cooled down

Sedimentary Rocks like limestone or chalk

Some carbon trapped as **fossil fuels**

oxygen built up very slowly

Oceans

oxygen O_2 (21%)   nitrogen N_2 (78%)

Our Atmosphere Now

▶ Carbon dioxide

- The level of carbon dioxide in the atmosphere is kept constant by the carbon cycle.
- However, our burning of fossil fuels releases vast amounts of carbon dioxide into the atmosphere.
- As industrialisation increases, the oceans can no longer cope with the volumes of carbon dioxide (a 'greenhouse gas') produced.
- The percentage of CO_2 in the air has grown from 0.028% to nearer 0.04% over the last 200 years.
- Most people are getting more and more concerned about the threat of global warming and its link to rising levels of CO_2.

More in **Chemistry for You**, pages 56–59, 300–321.

▶ Noble gases

A small proportion of the air is made up of noble gases – from Group 0 in the Periodic Table.

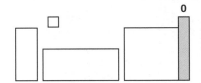

These gases are very unreactive.

Uses

Helium – used in balloons (because of its very low density).

Neon – used in electric discharge tubes (to give the bright advertising signs seen in cities.

Argon – used inside light bulbs (to stop the hot metal filament reacting with oxygen in air).

Earth and its atmosphere

Homework Questions

1 Los Angeles, in America, frequently gets earthquakes. The UK very rarely gets earthquakes. Why is this? *(1 mark)*

2 Which part of the Earth is the lithosphere? *(1 mark)*

3 Why was Wegener's theory of continental drift eventually accepted as being correct? *(1 mark)*

4 When the Earth was created, billions of years ago, where did the atmosphere come from? *(1 mark)*

5 How did the first oxygen gas get into the Earth's atmosphere? *(1 mark)*

6 Explain how the Earth's oceans were formed. *(1 mark)*

7 (a) Today, the Earth's atmosphere contains a small, almost constant, amount of carbon dioxide. Burning fossil fuels releases huge amounts of carbon dioxide into the air, so how can the percentage of carbon dioxide remain almost constant? *(1 mark)*

   (b) The amount of carbon dioxide in the air has however increased quite a bit since about 1850 (from 0.028% to almost 0.04%). Why is this? *(1 mark)*

   (c) The increase in carbon dioxide levels is causing great anxiety among scientists across the world. Why are people very worried about increasing carbon dioxide levels in the air? *(1 mark)*

8 Helium, neon and argon are sometimes called the 'Inert gases'. What does this mean? *(1 mark)*

9 (a) What do we call the group in the Periodic Table which contains helium, neon and argon? *(1 mark)*

   (b) Find out the names of three other elements in this group. *(3 marks)*

$\overline{14}$ marks

Examination Question

The bar chart shows the composition of the Earth's atmosphere today, and as it was billions of years ago.

Use information from the bar chart to describe how the atmosphere today is different from the atmosphere of billions of years ago.

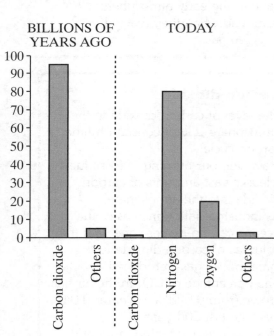

....

....

....

.... *(2 marks)*

$\overline{2}$ marks

Multiple Choice Examination Questions

1 Which of the following is correct?
The Earth is made up of the crust, the mantle and:

A a solid inner core, and solid outer core.

B a molten inner core, and molten outer core.

C a solid inner core, and molten outer core.

D a molten inner core, and solid outer core.

2 Volcanoes and earthquakes normally occur:

A south of the equator

B north of the equator

C near a tectonic plate boundary

D in or near countries with a hot climate

3 Wegener's theory of continental drift was not accepted at first because:

A his ideas were wrong.

B he could not prove the theory was right.

C we already knew about plate movements.

D rocks and fossils were found everywhere.

4 Which gas is **not** formed by volcanic action?

A oxygen

B water vapour

C ammonia

D carbon dioxide

5 One theory suggests that tectonic plates move on convection currents generated by heat from radioactive rocks. In which part of the Earth are these convection currents thought to be set up?

A outer core

B inner core

C crust

D mantle

6 The process by which green plants absorb carbon dioxide gas is called:

A respiration

B perspiration

C oxidation

D photosynthesis

7 The atmosphere today is mostly made up of:

	oxygen (%)	nitrogen (%)	argon (%)
A	21	78	0.9
B	21	0.9	78
C	0.9	78	21
D	0.9	21	78

8 Oxygen, nitrogen and argon make up 99.9% of the atmosphere, and the other 0.1% is:

A mostly steam

B mostly hydrogen

C a mixture of several gases

D a mixture of methane and hydrogen

9 Helium can be used in balloons because:

A it has a low density

B it is very reactive

C it is an inert gas

D it is a flammable gas

10 Carbon dioxide is sometimes called a 'greenhouse gas' because it:

A is a useful energy source for houses

B traps the Earth's heat in the air

C is found in houses with green plants

D can be used to heat greenhouses

Answers on page 110

Getting the Grades – Alkenes and polymers

Try this question, then compare your answer with the two examples opposite ▶

A propene molecule can be represented by the structure shown below.

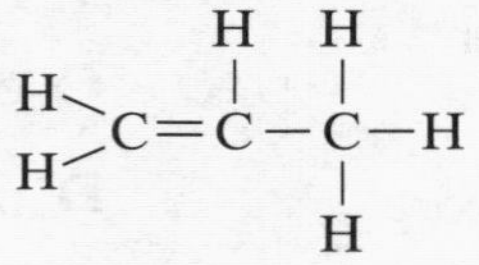

$$\begin{array}{c} H \quad H \\ | \quad | \\ \begin{matrix} H \\ \diagdown \\ H \diagup \end{matrix} C=C-C-H \\ | \\ H \end{array}$$

(a) Propene is made by cracking hydrocarbons obtained from crude oil.

 (i) How does cracking change hydrocarbon molecules?

 .... *(1 mark)*

 (ii) What conditions are needed for cracking to take place?

 .... *(2 marks)*

(b) The propene molecule is *unsaturated*.

 (i) What does the term *unsaturated* mean?

 .... *(1 mark)*

 (ii) Describe a chemical test to show that propene is unsaturated.

 ....

 .... *(2 marks)*

(c) This equation represents the *polymerisation* of propene.

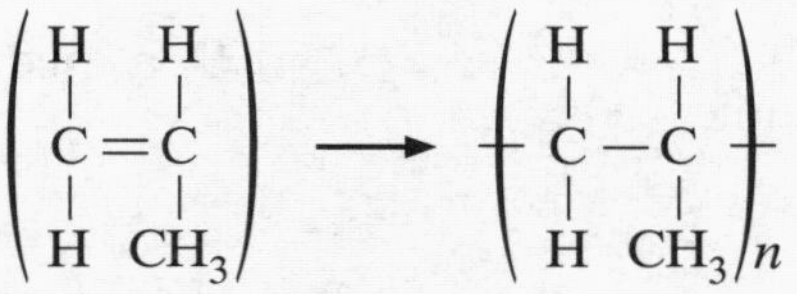

$$n\left(\begin{array}{c} H \quad H \\ | \quad | \\ C=C \\ | \quad | \\ H \quad CH_3 \end{array}\right) \longrightarrow \left(\begin{array}{c} H \quad H \\ | \quad | \\ C-C \\ | \quad | \\ H \quad CH_3 \end{array}\right)_n$$

 (i) Name the polymer produced by this reaction.

 .... *(1 mark)*

 (ii) Explain the meaning of the term polymerisation.

 ....

 .... *(2 marks)*

 (iii) Explain why the disposal of this polymer can cause environmental problems.

 ....

 ....

 ....

 .... *(2 marks)*

11 marks

GRADE 'A' ANSWER

(a) (i) Cracking splits large hydrocarbon molecules into smaller more useful molecules. ✓

(ii) The hydrocarbons are heated so that they turn into a vapour. ✓
This vapour is then passed over a hot catalyst. ✓

(b) (i) It has a double bond. ✓

(ii) Shake the propene with bromine water. The bromine water turns colourless. ✓✗

A good answer would state that the bromine water changes from orange/yellow to colourless.

(c) (i) poly(propene) ✓

(ii) The reaction in which many small molecules (monomers) ✓ join together to form a polymer. ✓

(iii) The polymer is non-biodegradable. ✓ This means that it takes up valuable space in land-fill sites. ✓

10 marks = Grade A answer

▶ **Improve your Grades   A up to A***

This is a very good answer with only one small piece of information missing. A grade A* answer should include this level of fine detail. Your examination paper will contain questions which ask about environmental issues related to Chemistry. Part (c)(iii) asks about the problems caused by the disposal of polymers. Be prepared to give detailed answers to such questions. You might consider:

- The littering of the countryside.
- The problems caused by burning plastics.
- The need for many waste disposal sites to take large quantities of plastic waste which does not biodegrade.

GRADE 'C' ANSWER

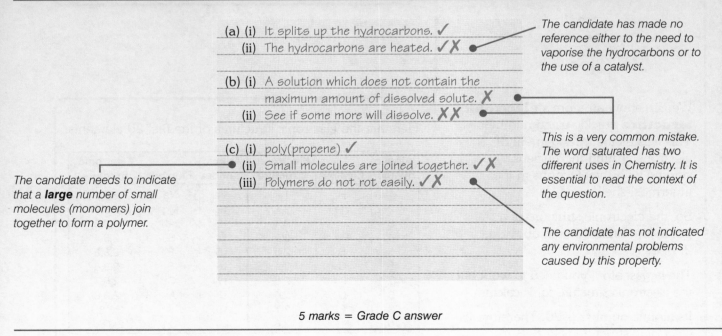

(a) (i) It splits up the hydrocarbons. ✓

(ii) The hydrocarbons are heated. ✓✗

The candidate has made no reference either to the need to vaporise the hydrocarbons or to the use of a catalyst.

(b) (i) A solution which does not contain the maximum amount of dissolved solute. ✗

(ii) See if some more will dissolve. ✗✗

This is a very common mistake. The word saturated has two different uses in Chemistry. It is essential to read the context of the question.

(c) (i) poly(propene) ✓

(ii) Small molecules are joined together. ✓✗

(iii) Polymers do not rot easily. ✓✗

*The candidate needs to indicate that a **large** number of small molecules (monomers) join together to form a polymer.*

The candidate has not indicated any environmental problems caused by this property.

5 marks = Grade C answer

▶ **Improve your Grades   C up to B**

Remember:
A **saturated** compound does not contain any double bonds in its **molecules**.
An **unsaturated** compound contains double bonds in its **molecules**. (Do not confuse this with saturated **solutions**.)
You should be able to draw diagrams like the one shown at the start of the question to show the structure of alkanes and alkenes.

ATOMIC STRUCTURE

▶ ThinkAbout:

1. Name the three types of sub-atomic particle found inside atoms.
2. Which of the sub-atomic particles carries a negative charge?
3. Which of the sub-atomic particles is neutral?
4. An atom has a mass number of 7 and an atomic number of 3. How many of each type of sub-atomic particle does it contain?
5. What is the difference between the atoms of isotopes of an element?

▶ Electronic structures

The electrons whizz around the nucleus in **shells** (or **energy levels**).
The first shell holds up to **2** electrons.
The second shell can hold up to **8** electrons.
The third shell holds **8** electrons.

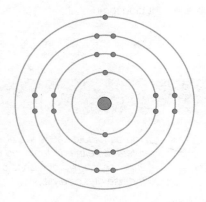

Here are the properties of the sub-atomic particles found in atoms:

Particle	Charge	Mass (in atomic mass units)
proton	1+	1
neutron	0	1
electron	1−	0 (almost)

We can show an atom's **electronic structure** quickly using numbers. This tells us the arrangement of electrons around the nucleus, starting with the electrons in the innermost shell.

So, the electronic structure of a potassium atom (shown above) is 2, 8, 8, 1.

The largest atom you need to work out the electronic structure for is calcium.

Its atomic number is 20. Therefore its electronic structure is 2, 8, 8, 2.

Here are the electronic structures of the first 20 elements:

Atomic number	Element	Electronic structure	Atomic number	Element	Electronic structure
1	H	1	11	Na	2,8,1
2	He	2	12	Mg	2,8,2
3	Li	2,1	13	Al	2,8,3
4	Be	2,2	14	Si	2,8,4
5	B	2,3	15	P	2,8,5
6	C	2,4	16	S	2,8,6
7	N	2,5	17	Cl	2,8,7
8	O	2,6	18	Ar	2,8,8
9	F	2,7	19	K	2,8,8,1
10	Ne	2,8	20	Ca	2,8,8,2

▶ Atomic number

> The **atomic number** tells us how many protons there are in an atom.

This also equals the number of electrons. That's because atoms themselves are neutral, therefore they must have the same number of protons (+) as electrons (−).

Mass number

> The **mass number** tells us the number of protons plus neutrons.

We can show these like this:

mass number $\longrightarrow$ $^{14}_{7}\text{N}$
atomic number $\longrightarrow$

You have 13 protons and 14 neutrons. Your mass number is 27. Try Weight-watchers Al.

SPEAK YOUR MASS

▶ Isotopes

The atoms of any particular element always contain the same number of electrons. However, their number of neutrons can differ.

Isotopes of an element contain different numbers of neutrons. Look at the examples below:

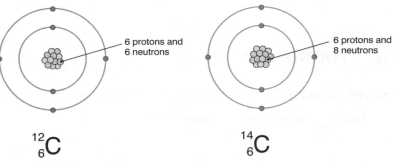

6 protons and 6 neutrons

$^{12}_{6}\text{C}$

6 protons and 8 neutrons

$^{14}_{6}\text{C}$

As you can see from this example:

> **Isotopes** of an element have the same atomic number but different mass numbers.

Isotopes are a bit like Easter eggs which have the same chocolate shell, but different numbers of sweets inside !

▶ Relative atomic mass

The relative atomic mass, A_r, of an element takes into account the proportion of its different isotopes in a naturally-occurring sample. Their mass is compared to the mass of the ^{12}C isotope.

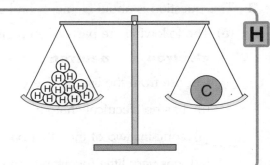

H

More in **Chemistry for You**, pages 30–38.

Atomic structure

Homework Questions

1 At least three different scientists are credited with the discovery of the atomic particles proton, neutron and electron. Find out when these particles were discovered, and the names of the scientists who made the discovery. *(3 marks)*

2 (a) Which two particles are found in the nucleus? *(2 marks)*
(b) Which particle orbits the nucleus? *(1 mark)*

3 Work out the electronic structures of these elements. *Hint:* first find out the atomic numbers!
(a) potassium   (b) carbon   (c) sulfur   (d) argon   *(4 marks)*

4 Copy and complete this table of the sub-atomic particles:

Particle name	Mass of particle	Charge
electron		
	1	+1
neutron		

(5 marks)

5 Why isn't the mass of each particle in the table given in grams? *(1 mark)*

6 Explain the difference between the terms 'atomic number' and 'mass number'. *(2 marks)*

7 Copy and complete: Isotopes of an ... contain the same number of ... and ... but different numbers of ... . *(4 marks)*

22 marks

Examination Questions

1 The diagram represents an atom. Choose words from the list to label the diagram.

electron   ion   neutron   nucleus

A ....
B ....
C ....
proton

(3 marks)

3 marks

2 This question is about elements and atoms.

(a) The following are parts of an atom:

electron   neutron   nucleus   proton

Choose from the list the one which:

(i)   has no electrical charge;   ....

(ii) contains two of the other particles;   ....

(iii) has very little (negligible) mass.   ....   *(3 marks)*

(b) Scientists have been able to make new elements in nuclear reactors. One of these new elements is fermium. An atom of fermium is represented by the symbol below.

$$^{257}_{100}\textbf{Fm}$$

    (i) How many protons does this atom contain? ....

    (ii) How many neutrons does this atom contain? .... *(2 marks)*

5

marks

3 John Dalton wrote these statements in 1808.
- "All substances are made of a vast number of extremely small particles called atoms."
- "Every particle of water is like every other particle of water, every particle of hydrogen is like every other particle of hydrogen, etc."

Dalton thought that all atoms of an element were exactly the same. We now know that it is possible to have atoms of the same element but with different mass numbers.
The diagrams represent two atoms of hydrogen.

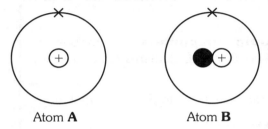

    Atom **A**   Atom **B**

(a) State, in terms of particles, how these two atoms are different.

....

.... *(2 marks)*

(b) Complete this sentence by choosing the correct word from the box.

ions	**isotopes**	**molecules**	**protons**

Atoms of the same element which have different mass numbers are called

.... *(1 mark)*

3

marks

4 The electronic structure of a sodium atom can be represented as in the diagram below.

Sodium atom

Draw a similar diagram for a fluorine atom. Use the Data Sheet on page 118 to help you.

1

mark

(1 mark)

Answers on page 111

Bonding

> ## ThinkAbout:

1. Describe the movement of the particles in a solid.
2. What happens to the particles in a solid as they are warmed up?
3. What is the difference between an atom and an ion?
4. Explain what a chemical compound is.
5. Write the formula of the ions found in sodium chloride.
6. How many electrons are shared in a single covalent bond?

> ## Ionic bonding

Metals bond to non-metals in **ionic compounds**. (A compound is a substance in which atoms of two, or more, elements are chemically combined.)

The metal atom gives one, or more, electrons to the non-metal atom.

This happens as the elements react together.

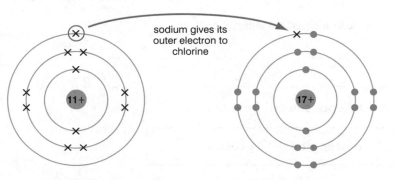

sodium gives its outer electron to chlorine

The charged particles formed are called **ions**.

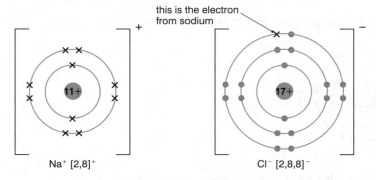

this is the electron from sodium

Na⁺ [2,8]⁺   Cl⁻ [2,8,8]⁻

Opposites attract !

The electrostatic attractions between oppositely charged ions are called **ionic bonds**.

- Metal atoms form positive ions (for example, Na^+, Mg^{2+}, Al^{3+}).
- Atoms of non-metals form negative ions (for example, Cl^-, O^{2-}).

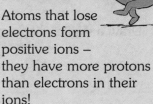

Take care:

Atoms that lose electrons form positive ions – they have more protons than electrons in their ions!

Answers: 1. they vibrate. 2. they vibrate more vigorously (quickly) 3. atoms are neutral, whereas ions are charged 4. a substance made of two or more types of atom bonded together 5. Na⁺ and Cl⁻ 6. 2 electrons

48

▶ Covalent bonding

Atoms of non-metals can bond to each
other by **sharing pairs of electrons**.

This is **covalent bonding**.

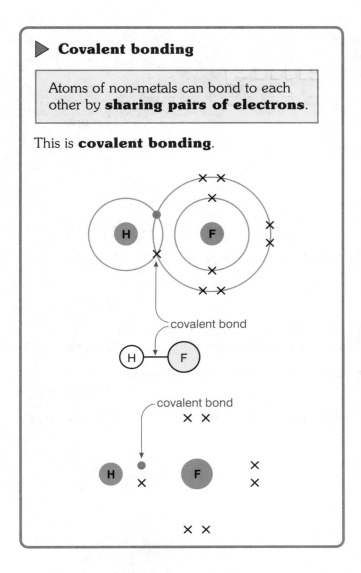

▶ More covalent bonding

Look at the bonding in methane, CH_4, below:

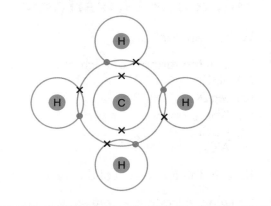

▶ Double covalent bond

Look at the double covalent bond in oxygen
below:

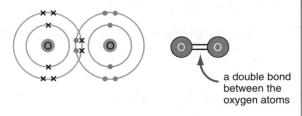

Notice that a single covalent bond contains
a pair of electrons and a double bond has
2 pairs.

H

▶ Metallic bonding

The atoms (or positive ions) in a metal are held to each other by
a 'sea' of free electrons. These **delocalised** electrons:
- hold the atoms (or ions) together in giant structures,
- can transfer energy through the metal when it conducts electricity or heat,
- let the atoms (or ions) slip over each other when the metal is hit or stretched.

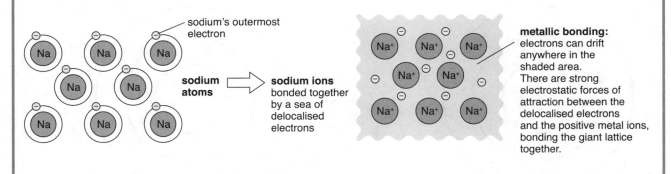

More in *Chemistry for You*,
pages 248–251, 256–257, 268.

Bonding

Homework Questions

1 What is an 'ion'? *(1 mark)*

2 What is the formula of each of the ions present in:
(a) NaCl
(b) MgO
(c) KBr
(d) $CaCl_2$
(e) $AlCl_3$ *(5 marks)*

3 Explain the two essential differences between ionic and covalent bonding. *(2 marks)*

4 Draw an electron diagram showing how the bond is formed in a molecule of hydrogen chloride gas (HCl). *(1 mark)*

5 Draw an electron diagram showing the bonding in a molecule of carbon dioxide, CO_2.
(*Hint:* carbon atoms have 6 electrons, oxygen atoms have eight electrons.) *(1 mark)*

6 Explain what happens to the delocalised electrons in a metal, such as copper, when it conducts an electric current. *(1 mark)*

7 Explain the essential differences between ionic bonding and metallic bonding. *(2 marks)*

13
marks

Examination Questions

1 Many foods contain chemical additives.
A tin of red kidney beans contains calcium chloride as a firming agent.

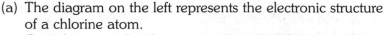

Calcium chloride is an ionic compound which contains calcium ions (Ca^{2+}) and chloride ions (Cl^-).

(a) The diagram on the left represents the electronic structure of a chlorine atom.
Complete a similar diagram on the right to represent a chloride ion.

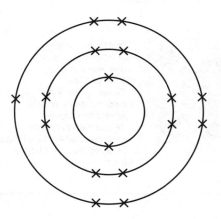 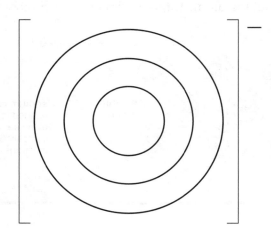

(1 mark)

(b) Explain how a calcium **atom** changes into a calcium **ion** which has a 2+ charge.

....

....

....

.... *(1 mark)*

2   Uranium metal can be produced by reacting uranium hexafluoride with calcium:

$$UF_6 + 3Ca \longrightarrow 3CaF_2 + U$$

Describe how calcium and fluorine bond together to form calcium fluoride. The electron arrangement of each atom is shown.

Calcium atom

Fluorine atom

....

....

....

....

.... *(5 marks)*

3   Fluorine is a very useful element. It is placed in Group 7 of the Periodic Table.
Use your knowledge of the elements in Group 7 to help you answer these questions.
Information in the Data Sheet (see page 118) may help you with this question.
Fluorine reacts with the non-metal sulfur to make sulfur hexafluoride (SF_6).

(a) What type of bonding would you expect in sulfur hexafluoride?

.... *(1 mark)*

(b) Explain the reason for your answer to part (a).

....

....

.... *(2 marks)*

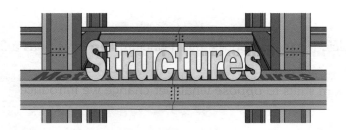

Structures

ThinkAbout:

1. Which of these substances has the lowest boiling point?
   water, iron, oxygen, zinc, petrol
2. Which of these substances conducts electricity in the solid state?
   gold, poly(ethene), rubber, aluminium, sodium

3. When water boils, what happens to the covalent bonds between the hydrogen and oxygen atoms?
4. When salt (sodium chloride) melts, what happens to the ionic bonds between sodium and chloride ions?

Structure and properties of ionic compounds

The ions form regular structures called **giant ionic lattices**.

Cl⁻ ion
Na⁺ ion

- There are strong electrostatic forces of attraction between millions of oppositely charged ions. These forces act in all directions.
- So ionic compounds have high melting points.

Ionic compounds don't conduct electricity when they are solid. However, they do if you melt them or dissolve them in water. The ions are then free to move around and carry the charge through the liquid.

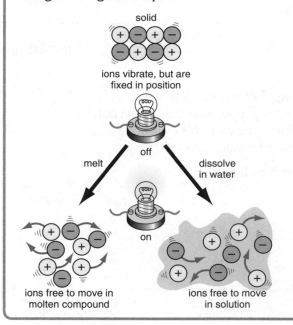

solid

ions vibrate, but are fixed in position

off

melt

dissolve in water

on

ions free to move in molten compound

ions free to move in solution

Properties of simple molecular substances

Many **covalently bonded** substances are made up of small individual molecules (for example, water). These have relatively low melting points and boiling points.

The simple molecules also carry no overall electrical charge so they do not conduct electricity.

Explaining low melting and boiling points

H

The forces *between* molecules (intermolecular forces) are relatively weak. So it is quite easy to separate the molecules from each other.

Look at the diagram below:

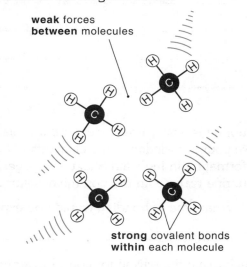

weak forces **between** molecules

strong covalent bonds **within** each molecule

Answers:
1. oxygen 2. gold, aluminium, sodium
3. nothing happens (*no* covalent bonds are broken)
4. the ionic bonds are broken

▶ Properties of substances with giant covalent structures

Other substances with covalent bonds have **giant covalent structures** (sometimes known as **macromolecules**).
These have very high melting points (for example, diamond, silica and graphite).

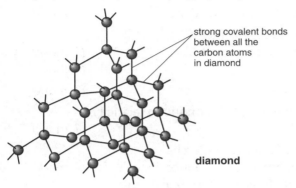

strong covalent bonds between all the carbon atoms in diamond

diamond

To melt these substances we have to break millions of strong covalent bonds.

Another form of carbon is graphite. Look at its structure below:

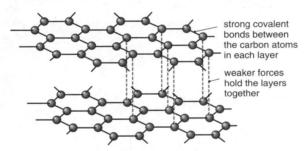

strong covalent bonds between the carbon atoms in each layer

weaker forces hold the layers together

Graphite is soft and slippery because the layers of carbon atoms can slide over each other.

▶ Nanoscience

This new technology involves very small groups of atoms. The structures only measure between 1 and 100 nanometres (nm), where $1 \text{ nm} = 10^{-9}$ m. These tiny structures have different properties to the bulk substance. For any given volume they have a huge surface area which is why new applications might include:

- superfast computers,
- catalysts,
- new coatings,
- highly selective sensors (that will help detect diseases),
- stronger and lighter building materials.

▶ Properties of metals

The atoms in metals are arranged in layers. These layers can slip past each other when we apply a force. That's why metals can be bent and shaped:

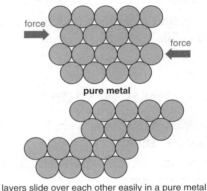

force

force

pure metal

layers slide over each other easily in a pure metal

▶ Why graphite conducts [H]

Normally covalently bonded substances do not conduct electricity in any state. However, graphite is the exception.

Notice that each carbon atom in graphite is only bonded to 3 other atoms. (Each atom in diamond forms the usual 4 covalent bonds.)
This leaves one electron from each carbon atom to drift along graphite's layers. These **delocalised** electrons enable graphite to conduct electricity.

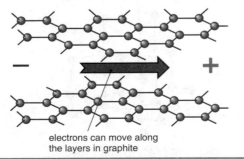

electrons can move along the layers in graphite

▶ Explaining the properties of metals [H]

Metals have giant structures. The strong electrostatic attraction between the delocalised electrons and positive metal ions (see bottom of page 49) means that most metals have high melting points. The 'sea of delocalised electrons' explains why metals are good conductors of heat and electricity.

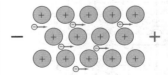

Delocalised electrons move towards the positive charge. These free electrons can also transfer heat through metals quickly.

More in **Chemistry for You**, pages 252–253, 258–267, 268, 271, 274–275, 336–337.

Structures

Homework Questions

1 Why is there no such thing as a 'molecule' of sodium chloride? *(1 mark)*

2 Explain why no ionic compound conducts electricity when solid, but they all do when molten. *(1 mark)*

3 Why is it that most simple covalent molecules do not conduct electricity? *(1 mark)*

4 (a) Which of these solutions would you expect to conduct electricity?
      ethanol   propanone   ether   potassium nitrate   petrol *(1 mark)*
  (b) Give a reason for your answer to part (a). *(1 mark)*

5 Why is diamond sometimes referred to as a macromolecule? *(1 mark)*

6 Diamond and graphite are both made from carbon, yet graphite conducts electricity, but diamond does not. Explain why this is. *(1 mark)*

7 Nano-technology is a new and fast developing area of science research.
  (a) Explain why these new areas of science are sometimes called 'nanoscience'. *(1 mark)*
  (b) Look up nano-technology in a textbook or use the Internet, and explain the meaning of the term 'nanobot'. *(1 mark)*
  (c) Explain how 'nanobots' could be of enormous benefit to people in the future. *(1 mark)*
  (d) Some other terms you might research are 'nanocluster' and 'nanotube'. Explain what these are and say how they could be used in the future. *(2 marks)*

8 Most metals have high melting points and are excellent conductors of electricity. Why is this? *(2 marks)*

14 marks

Examination Questions

[H] **1** Chlorine will combine with the non-metal element, carbon, by sharing electrons.

The carbon tetrachloride which is produced has a low boiling point.

Explain, as fully as you can, why this is.

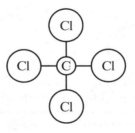

....

....

.... *(3 marks)*

3 marks

2 The diagrams show the giant structures of sodium chloride and diamond.

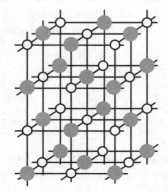

sodium chloride (melting point 801°C)

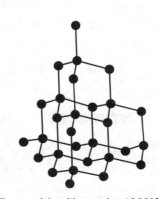

diamond (melting point 4800°C)

54

(a) By reference to the detailed structure of sodium chloride, explain fully why:

(i) sodium chloride has quite a high melting point,

....

....

.... *(2 marks)*

(ii) solid sodium chloride melts when it is heated strongly,

....

....

.... *(2 marks)*

(iii) molten sodium chloride will conduct electricity.

....

.... *(1 mark)*

(b) By reference to the detailed structure of diamond, explain why the melting point of diamond, is higher than that of sodium chloride.

....

....

....

.... *(2 marks)*

———
7
marks

3 The diagram represents part of the structure of graphite.

Use your knowledge and understanding of the structure of graphite to explain why graphite can be used:

(a) in the 'leads' of pencils;

....

....

....

.... *(3 marks)*

[H]   (b) as an electrical conductor.

....

....

....

.... *(3 marks)*

———
6
marks

mass ÷ moles

$1 \times A_r$ of Ca = 40

Chemical calculations

no. of moles = $\dfrac{mass}{R.F.M.}$

Relative formula mass of NO_2

The relative atomic mass (R.A.M.) is given the symbol A_r. (See page 45.)

We work out the relative formula mass (M_r) of a substance by adding up the A_r values of each element in the ratio shown by the formula. (See $CaCO_3$ example below.)

We can talk about how much substance we have using a quantity called 'the **mole**'.

> We say that the relative formula mass (M_r) of a substance, in grams, contains **one mole** of that substance.

To work out how many atoms are present in a given mass:

> **no. of moles** = $\dfrac{\textbf{mass}}{\textbf{R.A.M. } (A_r)}$

Example 1

How many moles of carbon atoms are there in 2.4 g of carbon (A_r of C = 12)?

Number of moles = $\dfrac{2.4}{12}$ = **0.2 moles of carbon**

To work out the mass of atoms present:

> **mass = no. of moles × R.A.M. (A_r)**

To work out the number of moles of substance present:

> **no. of moles** = $\dfrac{\textbf{mass}}{\textbf{R.F.M. } (M_r)}$

where M_r **is the relative formula mass** (R.F.M.) of a substance.

H

▶ Working out the formula

> The simplest ratio of the numbers of moles of each element present in a compound is called its **empirical formula.**

Example 3

A compound of carbon and oxygen contains 3 g of carbon and 8 g of oxygen. What is its empirical formula?

Work out the ratio of moles, C : O

Moles of carbon = $\dfrac{3}{12}$ = 0.25 moles

Moles of oxygen = $\dfrac{8}{16}$ = 0.5 moles

C : O ratio is 0.25 : 0.5 = 1 : 2

Therefore the empirical formula (simplest whole number ratio) is CO_2.

Example 2

Work out the relative formula mass (R.F.M.) of calcium carbonate, $CaCO_3$ (A_r: Ca = 40, C = 12, O = 16):

$1 \times A_r$ of Ca	= (1 × 40)	40
$1 \times A_r$ of C	= (1 × 12)	12
$3 \times A_r$ of O	= (3 × 16) =	+48
M_r of $CaCO_3$		**100**

To work out the mass of substance present:

> **mass = no. of moles × R.F.M. (M_r)**

Take care:

Write down the steps in your calculation – then you can gain some marks even if your final answer is wrong!

▷ Percentage composition

The **percentage composition** of a compound gives us the proportion of each element present by mass, expressed in percentages.

percentage of an element in a compound
$= \dfrac{\text{mass of that element in 1 mole of the compound}}{\text{relative formula mass of the compound}} \times 100$

Example 4

What is the percentage by mass of nitrogen in nitrogen dioxide, NO_2
(A_r of N = 14, O = 16)?

Mass of N in one mole of NO_2 = 14 g

Relative formula mass of NO_2 = 14 + (2 × 16) = 46 g

% of N in NO_2 = $\left(\frac{14}{46}\right) \times 100$ = **30.4%**

▷ Percentage yield

In many reactions in industry we do not manage to get the calculated amount of useful product. That's because:

- some reactions are reversible. (See next page.)
- some product is lost when separating it from the reaction mixture.
- some unexpected reactions may take place.

▷ Calculating percentage yield

We can calculate percentage yield using this equation:

percentage yield =
$\dfrac{\text{actual mass of product collected}}{\begin{array}{c}\text{mass of product that could}\\\text{be formed in theory}\end{array}} \times 100$

▷ Atom economy

This tells us how much of the starting materials end up as useful products in industrial processes. The higher the atom economy, the less wastage and pollution, and the more profitable the process is.

▷ Calculating atom economy

We can calculate percentage atom economy using this equation:

% atom economy = $\dfrac{\text{mass of useful product}}{\begin{array}{c}\text{total mass of reactants}\\\text{(or products)}\end{array}} \times 100$

▷ Reacting masses [H]

We can use balanced equations to calculate the masses of reactants and products in a chemical reaction.

Example 5

Lead(II) oxide, PbO, is heated with carbon to produce lead according to the equation:

$$2PbO + C \longrightarrow 2Pb + CO_2$$

How much carbon is needed to just reduce 111.5 tonnes of lead(II) oxide?
(Pb = 207, C = 12, O = 16)

Step 1

From the balanced equation we can say that 2 moles of PbO react with 1 mole of C.

Step 2

Changing the moles to masses:
So 2 × (207 + 16) tonnes of PbO reacts with 12 tonnes of C.

446 tonnes of PbO reacts with 12 tonnes of C
  1 tonne of PbO reacts with $\frac{12}{446}$ tonnes of C

So 111. 5 tonnes of PbO reacts with
$\left(\frac{12}{446}\right) \times 111.5$ tonnes of C

∴ you need $\left(\frac{12}{446}\right) \times 111.5$ tonnes of carbon
= **3 tonnes of carbon**

More in *Chemistry for You*, pages 340–341, 346–353.

Chemical calculations

Homework Questions

1 In the chemical sense, what is a 'mole' of a substance? *(1 mark)*

2 How much would you have to weigh out in order to have one mole of:
(a) calcium (b) calcium oxide (CaO) (c) calcium chloride ($CaCl_2$)
[Ca = 40, O = 16, Cl = 35.5] *(3 marks)*

3 (a) Explain why the Relative Formula Mass (M_r) of calcium carbonate is 100. *(1 mark)*
(b) Calculate the M_r of sodium carbonate, Na_2CO_3 [Na = 23, C = 12, O = 16] *(1 mark)*
(c) If you had 10.6 g of sodium carbonate, how many moles would you have? *(1 mark)*
(d) How many grams is 0.5 mole of sodium carbonate? *(1 mark)*

4 Calculate the percentage by mass of nitrogen
(a) in ammonia NH_3 [N = 14, H = 1] (b) in ammonium nitrate NH_4NO_3 [O = 16] *(2 marks)*

H **5** In this equation: $2PbO + C \longrightarrow 2Pb + CO_2$
calculate the mass of lead which could be made from 446 tonnes of lead(ll) oxide.
[Pb = 207, O =16] *(1 mark)*

H **6** What is the mass of oxygen needed to react with magnesium ribbon to make 4 g of
magnesium oxide? $2Mg + O_2 \longrightarrow 2MgO$ [Mg = 24, O = 16] *(1 mark)*

H **7** In a chemical reaction, exactly 2.3 g of sodium was found to react with 3.55 g of chlorine.
Calculate the empirical formula of the compound formed. [Na = 23, Cl = 35.5] *(1 mark)*

$$\frac{}{13}$$ marks

Examination Questions

1 Calcium oxide (quicklime) is made by heating calcium carbonate (limestone).

calcium carbonate $\longrightarrow$ calcium oxide + carbon dioxide
100 g   ?   44 g

(a) 44 grams of carbon dioxide is produced when 100 grams of calcium carbonate is heated.
Calculate the mass of calcium oxide produced when 100 grams of calcium carbonate is heated.

.... mass ....g *(1 mark)*

(b) What mass of carbon dioxide could be made from 100 tonnes of calcium carbonate?

mass ....tonnes *(1 mark)*

$$\frac{}{2}$$ marks

2 The ore haematite contains iron oxide.
The chemical equation for the formation of iron is:

$$Fe_2O_3 \text{ (s)} + 3CO \text{ (g)} \longrightarrow 2Fe \text{ (s)} + 3CO_2 \text{ (g)}$$

(a) What is the name of the gas, CO?

.... *(1 mark)*

(b) Put a circle around the name of the type of reaction where oxygen is removed from a
compound.

decomposition   neutralisation   oxidation   reduction *(1 mark)*

(c) Calculate the relative formula mass of iron oxide, Fe_2O_3.
(Relative atomic masses: O = 16; Fe = 56)

....

....

Relative formula mass Fe_2O_3 = ... *(2 marks)*

$$\frac{}{4}$$ marks

H **3** Titanium is a transition metal used as pins and plates to support badly broken bones. Titanium is extracted from an ore that contains the mineral titanium oxide. This oxide is converted into titanium chloride. Titanium chloride is heated with sodium to form titanium metal. This reaction takes place in an atmosphere of a noble gas, such as argon.

$$4Na \text{ (s)} + TiCl_4 \text{ (l)} \longrightarrow Ti \text{ (s)} + 4NaCl \text{ (s)}$$

(a) Why is an atmosphere of a noble gas needed for this reaction?

....

.... *(1 mark)*

(b) Suggest why the sodium displaces titanium in this reaction.

....

.... *(1 mark)*

(c) Calculate the mass of titanium that can be extracted from 570 kg of titanium chloride.
(Relative atomic masses: Cl = 35.5; Ti = 48)

....

....

....

Mass of titanium = ... kg   *(3 marks)*

5
marks

H **4** The structure formula of a hydrazine molecule is shown opposite.

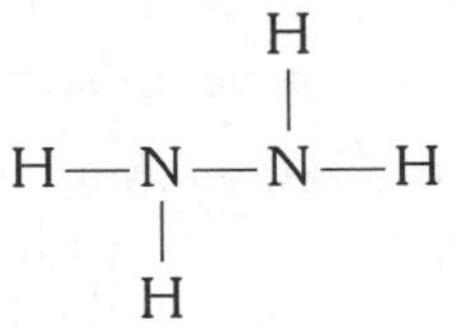

Hydrazine is produced from ammonia.
The equation which represents this reaction is:

$$2NH_3 + NaOCl \longrightarrow N_2H_4 + NaCl + H_2O$$

```
        H
        |
H — N — N — H
    |
    H
```

What mass of ammonia, NH_3, is needed to make 32 g of hydrazine, N_2H_4?
(Relative atomic masses: H = 1; N = 14)

....

.... *(2 marks)*

2
marks

H **5** This label has been taken from a box of aspirin.
The chemical name for aspirin is acetylsalicylic acid.

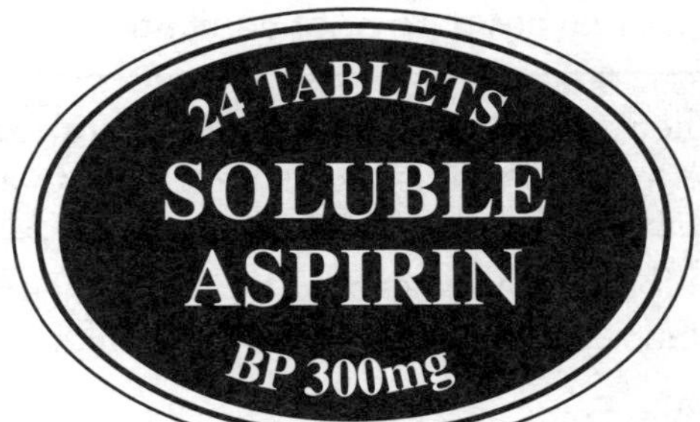

Acetylsalicylic acid contains 60.00% by mass of carbon, 4.48% hydrogen and 35.52% oxygen.

Use this information to show that the empirical formula of acetylsalicylic acid is $C_9H_8O_4$
Show clearly how you work out your final answer.
(Relative atomic masses: H = 1; C = 12; O = 16)

24 TABLETS
SOLUBLE ASPIRIN
BP 300mg

....

....

....

....

.... *(3 marks)*

3
marks

Reversible ⇄ Reactions

▶ ThinkAbout:

1. What is the main difference between a physical change and a reversible chemical change?

2. What do you see if you add too much acid to an alkaline solution containing universal indicator, and then add too much alkali?

3. a) How can you test for the presence of water using anhydrous copper sulfate?
   b) Give another chemical test for the presence of water.
   c) How could you show that the liquid was pure water?

▶ Examples of reversible reactions

Some reactions are **reversible**.

The reactants form the products, but the products can also react together to re-form the reactants:

$$\boxed{\text{reactants} \rightleftharpoons \text{products}}$$

- The test for water (white anhydrous copper sulfate turns blue) is a reversible reaction.
- The breakdown and formation of ammonium chloride is reversible:

$$\text{ammonium chloride} \rightleftharpoons \text{ammonia} + \text{hydrogen chloride}$$
$$NH_4Cl \text{ (s)} \rightleftharpoons NH_3 \text{ (g)} + HCl \text{ (g)}$$
a white solid   *colourless gases*

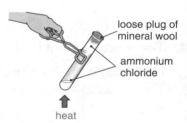

loose plug of mineral wool

ammonium chloride

heat

When the white ammonium chloride powder is heated it decomposes. It gives off ammonia and hydrogen chloride gases. On the cool part of the test-tube, the gases re-combine to form the white solid again.

H

▶ Dynamic equilibrium

In a closed system, nothing can escape. So we have reactants and products available to react. Eventually the reaction mixture reaches a point of equilibrium.

> When a reaction is in a state of **dynamic equilibrium**, the forward rate is the same as the reverse rate of reaction.

DOWN ESCALATOR

DYNAMIC EQUILIBRIUM

Therefore there appears to be no change in the quantities of substances present in the reacting mixture.

eg. $A + B \rightleftharpoons C + D$

All four substances (A, B, C and D) will be present in fixed proportions once equilibrium has been reached.

Answers:

1. new substances are formed in reversible chemical changes but not in physical changes
2. purple → red → purple again
3. a) it turns blue if water is present
   b) blue cobalt chloride turns pink
   c) it would boil at 100°C

▶ Making ammonia – The Haber process

Although almost 80% of the air is nitrogen gas, most plants can't use this directly to help them grow. So we add nitrogen-based **fertilisers** to the soil.

These are soluble compounds that can be absorbed through the roots of a plant.

However, these fertilisers can cause pollution in our water supplies and in rivers.

Nitrogen is converted to ammonia (NH_3) in the **Haber process**:

$$\text{nitrogen} + \text{hydrogen} \rightleftharpoons \text{ammonia}$$
$$N_2\,(g) + 3H_2\,(g) \rightleftharpoons 2NH_3\,(g)$$

- The catalyst used is iron.
- The temperature is about 450°C.
- The pressure is about 200 atmospheres.

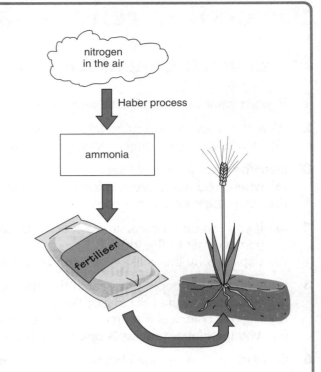

Any unreacted nitrogen and hydrogen are recycled to the reaction vessel.

The ammonia gas formed is cooled down. It condenses to a liquid that is removed and collected.

Look at the flow diagram of the process below:

The Haber process

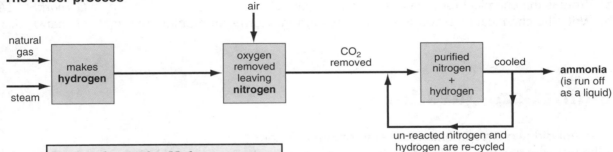

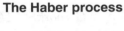

Facts about the Haber process
Raw materials

Air (for nitrogen)

Natural gas (to make hydrogen)

Steam (to make hydrogen and to generate high pressures)

Conditions

Temperature : about 450°C

Pressure : about 200 atmospheres

Catalyst : mainly iron

Why choose these conditions?

These conditions are chosen to give a reasonable yield of ammonia as quickly as possible. (See page 71.)

More in *Chemistry for You*, pages 220–222, 231.

Reversible reactions

Homework Questions

1 Explain what we mean by the term 'reversible reaction'. *(1 mark)*

2 Write the reversible equation for the chemical test for water (see ThinkAbout Q3):
(a) in words,   (b) using chemical formulae. *(2 marks)*

3 Describe what you would see:
(a) when solid ammonium chloride is heated, and then
(b) when the products are cooled. *(2 marks)*

4 (a) If you ran up an escalator at exactly the same speed as it was moving downwards, would
   you ever get to the top? *(1 mark)*
(b) Explain why this is like a reaction at 'dynamic equilibrium'. *(1 mark)*

5 Look up in a textbook, or research the Internet, and find out:
(a) when and where Fritz Haber lived,
(b) why his chemical research into ammonia interested his government at the time,
(c) why the Haber process is one of the most important reactions in the world. *(3 marks)*

6 80% of the air is nitrogen but most plants cannot use it directly to help them grow –
why not? *(1 mark)*

7 Why is a catalyst used in the Haber process? *(1 mark)*

8 One of the most common fertilisers is ammonium nitrate.
(a) What is the chemical formula of ammonium nitrate? *(1 mark)*
(b) Write the chemical equation to show how ammonia forms ammonium nitrate. *(1 mark)*

14 marks

Examination Questions

1 A student did two experiments using ammonium chloride.
In the first experiment the student heated a small amount of ammonium chloride in a test-tube.

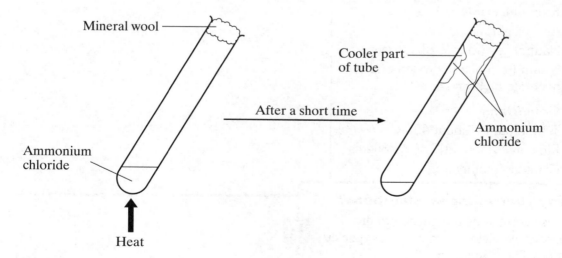

Mineral wool

Ammonium chloride

Heat

After a short time

Cooler part of tube

Ammonium chloride

Two reactions take place in the test-tube.

| **Reaction 1** | ammonium chloride $\longrightarrow$ ammonia + hydrogen chloride (colourless gases) |
| **Reaction 2** | ammonia + hydrogen chloride $\longrightarrow$ ammonium chloride |

(a) Complete the sentences by crossing out the **incorrect** word in each box.

Reaction **1** takes place at a ⟦high / low⟧ temperature.

Reaction **2** takes place at a ⟦high / low⟧ temperature. *(1 mark)*

(b) Draw a ring around the word which best describes reactions **1** and **2**.

combustion   displacement   oxidation   reduction   reversible *(1 mark)*

(c) Suggest a reason for the mineral wool at the top of the test-tube.

.... *(1 mark)*

3 marks

2 The flow chart below shows the main stages in the production of ammonium nitrate.

(a) (i) Name the two raw materials shown in the flow chart as **A** and **B**.

A .... **B** .... *(2 marks)*

(ii) What is the purpose of the iron in the reactor?

.... *(1 mark)*

(b) Balance the equation which represents the reaction that produces ammonia in the Haber process.

$$N_2 + ... H_2 \rightleftharpoons .... NH_3$$ *(1 mark)*

(c) Give the name of acid **C** which is added to the ammonia to make ammonium nitrate.

.... *(1 mark)*

(d) (i) Explain why farmers add ammonium nitrate to the soil.

....

....

.... *(2 marks)*

(ii) Explain how ammonium nitrate can cause pollution.

....

.... *(2 marks)*

9 marks

Rates of Reaction

▶ ThinkAbout:

1. Which of these factors will increase the rate of a reaction?
   A lowering the temperature
   B increasing the temperature
   C increasing the concentration of solutions
   D decreasing the concentration of solutions.

2. Which gas is given off when limestone reacts with dilute hydrochloric acid?
3. Which gas is given off when magnesium reacts with dilute hydrochloric acid?
4. Name a chemical reaction that takes place:
   a) very slowly
   b) very quickly.

▶ Measuring rates of reaction

We can measure rates of reaction by looking at how quickly products are formed.
We can also measure how quickly reactants are used up.

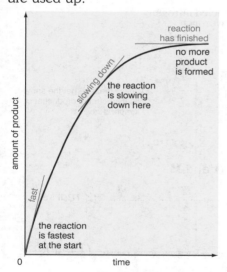

▶ Collision theory

We explain rates of reaction using the **collision theory**.

> Particles must collide, with sufficient energy, before a reaction can occur.

This minimum amount of energy is called the **activation energy**.

▶ Effect of surface area

> Rates of reaction are increased by increasing the **surface area** (using small pieces) of solids.

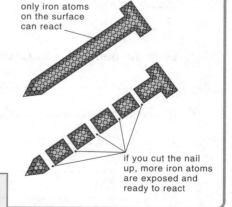

only iron atoms on the surface can react

if you cut the nail up, more iron atoms are exposed and ready to react

$$\text{Rate} = \frac{\text{amount of reactant used or product formed}}{\text{time}}$$

Effect of concentration

Rates of reaction are increased by increasing the **concentration** of solutions.

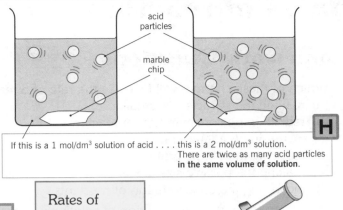

acid particles

marble chip

If this is a 1 mol/dm³ solution of acid . . . . this is a 2 mol/dm³ solution. There are twice as many acid particles **in the same volume of solution**.

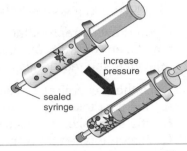

When we increase the concentration (or pressure in gas reactions), there are more particles in the same space so particles collide more often.

Take care:

When explaining the effect of concentration, don't just say that there are more particles – explain that there are more particles *in a given volume* and therefore more collisions *in a given time*.

Rates of reaction are increased by increasing the **pressure** of gases.

increase pressure

sealed syringe

H Equal volumes of any gas (at the same temperature and pressure) contain the same number of molecules.

Effect of temperature

Rates of reaction are increased by increasing the **temperature**.

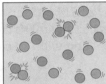

Reaction at 30°C

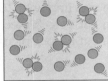

Reaction at 40°C

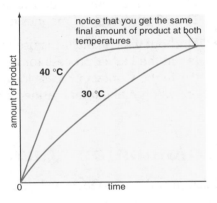

notice that you get the same final amount of product at both temperatures

amount of product

40 °C

30 °C

time

When we increase the temperature, the reacting particles gain more energy:
- They move around faster, so collisions are **more frequent**.
- The collisions are also **more energetic,** so are more likely to produce a reaction (more reacting particles will have energy that exceeds the **activation energy** for the reaction).

Catalysts

Rates of reaction are increased by using a **catalyst.** (That is, if you can find one for a particular reaction, as different reactions need different catalysts.)

NO CATALYST

over we go!

WITH CATALYST

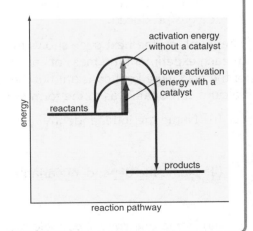

activation energy without a catalyst

lower activation energy with a catalyst

energy

reactants

products

reaction pathway

A catalyst can be used over and over again as it is not chemically changed itself at the end of the reaction.

More in *Chemistry for You*, pages 203–213, 218–219.

Rates of reaction

Homework Questions

1 Which of these changes will increase the rate of a reaction?
(a) making the particle size smaller
(b) reducing the concentration of reactants
(c) increasing the temperature
(d) reducing the temperature
(e) making the particle size bigger
(f) increasing the concentration of reactants.   *(2 marks)*

2 If you draw a graph of the amount of product formed in a reaction (on the y axis) against the time taken (on the x axis), how can you tell from the shape of the graph:
(a) where the reaction is fastest?   (b) when the reaction has reached completion?   *(2 marks)*

3 Place these chemical reactions in order, from slowest to quickest:
A the time taken for a freshly cut apple to go brown
B the time taken for a small piece of wood to decompose completely
C the time taken for a small piece of magnesium to react with dilute hydrochloric acid
D the time taken for a small iron nail in water to go completely rusty   *(1 mark)*

4 Why does increasing the pressure on gaseous reactants increase the rate of reaction? *(1 mark)*

5 Which reaction, from **A** to **D**, would you expect to produce the most hydrogen gas in the shortest time?   *(1 mark)*
A a 5 cm length of magnesium ribbon reacting with 10 cm^3 of 1M HCl (hydrochloric acid)
B a 5 cm length of magnesium ribbon reacting with 10 cm^3 of 1M HCl
C a 5 cm length of magnesium ribbon cut in to 5 pieces reacting with 10 cm^3 of 2M HCl
D a 5 cm length of magnesium ribbon cut in to 5 pieces reacting with 10 cm^3 of 1M HCl

6 Find out which catalyst is used:
(a) in the Haber process for making ammonia,
(b) in the Contact process for making sulfuric acid,
(c) when making margarine from vegetable oils.   *(3 marks)*

$$\frac{10}{\text{marks}}$$

Examination Question

Calcium carbonate reacts with dilute hydrochloric acid as shown in the equation below.

$$CaCO_3\ (s) + 2HCl\ (aq) \longrightarrow CaCl_2\ (aq) + H_2O\ (l) + CO_2\ (g)$$

The rate at which this reaction takes place can be studied by measuring the volume of carbon dioxide gas produced.

The graph on the next page shows the results of four experiments, **1** to **4**.
In each experiment the mass of calcium carbonate, the volume of acid and the concentration of the acid were kept constant but the temperature of the acid was changed each time. The calcium carbonate was in the form of small lumps of marble.

(a) (i) Name the independent variable in this investigation.

.... *(1 mark)*

(ii) Name the dependent variable.

.... *(1 mark)*

(iii) Name one control variable mentioned in this investigation.

.... *(1 mark)*

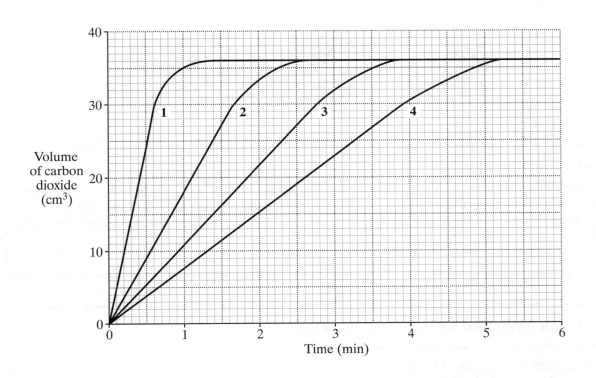

(b) Apart from altering the temperature, suggest two ways in which the reaction of calcium carbonate and hydrochloric acid could be speeded up.

1. ....

2. .... *(2 marks)*

(c) Which graph, **1** to **4**, shows the results of the experiment in which the acid had the highest temperature?

Experiment ....

Explain fully how you know.

....

....

....

.... *(2 marks)*

(d) (i) In experiment **2**, how does the rate of reaction after one minute compare with the rate of reaction after 2 minutes?

....

.... *(1 mark)*

(ii) Explain, as fully as you can, why the reaction rate changes during experiment **2**.

....

....

....

.... *(2 marks)*

10 marks

Answers on page 113

More about reactions

▶ **ThinkAbout:**

1. You are holding the bottom of a beaker containing two solutions that react together in an exothermic reaction. What do you feel?
2. Where do we get the energy our bodies need to survive?

3. In a reversible reaction, the forward reaction gives out 150 kJ/mol of energy. What energy do you think the reverse reaction will take in?

▶ **Exothermic and endothermic reactions**

> Reactions that give out energy, often as heat, are called **exothermic**.
> The temperature of the surroundings rises.

For example, combustion and most neutralisation reactions give out energy.

> Reactions that take in energy are called **endothermic**. The temperature of the surroundings falls.

For example, thermal decomposition reactions take in energy.

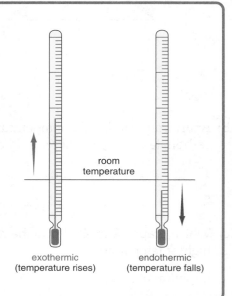

room temperature

exothermic
(temperature rises)

endothermic
(temperature falls)

▶ **Energy transfer in reversible reactions**

In a reversible reaction:
- If the forward reaction is exothermic, the reverse reaction is endothermic.
- If the forward reaction is endothermic, the reverse reaction is exothermic.

> In a reversible reaction, the amount of energy given out or taken in will be equal for the forward and reverse reactions.

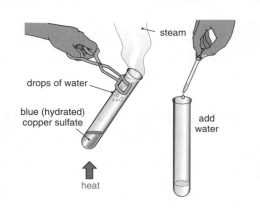

steam

drops of water

blue (hydrated) copper sulfate

add water

heat

An example is when we heat blue hydrated copper sulfate crystals:

hydrated copper sulfate (*+ heat energy*) ⇌ anhydrous copper sulfate + water
    blue crystals   *white powder*

We can use the reverse reaction as a test for water.

Answers: 1. it will feel warm/hot   2. food   3. 150 kJ/mol

▶ Affecting the position of equilibrium

> The position of equilibrium shifts to *oppose* whatever change we introduce to the system.

The various factors are shown below:

Changing concentration

- *Increasing* the concentration of one of the substances in the equilibrium mixture moves the position of equilibrium to favour the *opposite side*.

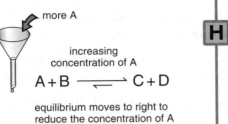

more A

increasing
concentration of A

$A + B \rightleftharpoons C + D$

equilibrium moves to right to
reduce the concentration of A

Effect of pressure

In reactions involving different numbers of gas molecules on either side of the equation:

- *Increasing* the pressure shifts the position of equilibrium to favour the side with the *least number* of gas molecules.
- *Decreasing* the pressure shifts the position of equilibrium to favour the side with the *greater number* of gas molecules.

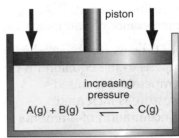

piston

increasing
pressure

$A(g) + B(g) \rightleftharpoons C(g)$

equilibrium moves to the side with
the least number of gas molecules
to reduce the pressure

Effect of temperature

- *Increasing* the temperature shifts the position of equilibrium to favour the *endothermic reaction*.
- *Decreasing* the temperature shifts the position of equilibrium to favour the *exothermic reaction*.

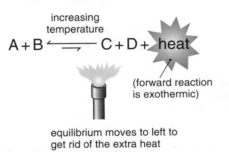

increasing
temperature

$A + B \rightleftharpoons C + D +$ heat

(forward reaction
is exothermic)

equilibrium moves to left to
get rid of the extra heat

Take care:

- Reversible reactions in industry are not always carried out at the highest possible temperature.

- If a high temperature favours the reactants, a temperature is chosen that is a compromise between a lower yield and a faster rate of reaction.

▶ Reversible reactions in industry

In industrial processes that involve reversible reactions, chemists have to balance the need for a reasonable yield with the need for a fast rate of reaction. For example, in the **Haber process**:

$$N_2\,(g) \; + \; 3H_2\,(g) \; \rightleftharpoons \; 2NH_3\,(g) \quad \Delta H = -92 \text{ kJ/mol (exothermic in forward direction)}$$

- A low temperature favours a high yield of ammonia, but at a slow rate. So a temperature of 450°C is chosen as a compromise between yield and rate.
- Iron is used as a catalyst to speed up the rate of reaction. But because it speeds up both the forward and reverse reaction, it doesn't affect the yield of ammonia.

> A **catalyst** speeds up the *rate* at which we reach equilibrium, but does not affect the position of equilibrium.

More in *Chemistry for You*, pages 194–195, 220, 223–225, 232–233.

More about reactions

Homework Questions

1 Explain what we mean by 'exothermic' and 'endothermic' when referring to chemical reactions. *(2 marks)*

2 New bonds are made during a chemical reaction. Will this be an exothermic or endothermic process? *(1 mark)*

[H] **3** In this reversible reaction, $P + Q \rightleftharpoons R + S$, what would happen to the equilibrium position if you added more of S to the mixture? *(1 mark)*

[H] **4** In this equilibrium reaction, $W + X \rightleftharpoons Y + Z$, the forward reaction is exothermic. What would happen to the equilibrium position if you cooled the mixture? *(1 mark)*

[H] **5** In this reversible reaction, $2SO_2 \text{ (g)} + O_2 \text{ (g)} \rightleftharpoons 2SO_3 \text{ (g)}$, what would happen to the equilibrium position if you increased the pressure on the mixture? *(1 mark)*

[H] **6** The Haber process for the production of ammonia is a very important industrial process. What happens to the equilibrium position when:
(a) the temperature is raised?
(b) the pressure is increased?
(c) the concentration of ammonia is decreased? *(3 marks)*

[H] **7** In the Haber process, a higher temperature of about 600°C would increase the rate of reaction, but in practice a lower temperature of about 450°C is used. Why is this? *(1 mark)*

[H] **8** What role do catalysts play in some equilibrium reactions? *(1 mark)*

$\dfrac{11}{\text{marks}}$

Examination Questions

1 The symbol equation below shows the reaction when methane burns in oxygen.

$$CH_4 + 2O_2 \longrightarrow CO_2 + 2H_2O$$

An energy level diagram for this reaction is shown opposite.

(a) Which chemical bonds are broken and which are formed during this reaction?

....

....

.... *(4 marks)*

(b) Explain the significance of x, y and z on the energy level diagram in terms of the energy transfers which occur when these chemical bonds are broken and formed.

....

....

....

....

.... *(5 marks)*

$\dfrac{9}{\text{marks}}$

2 The Haber process is used to make ammonia (NH_3) which is an important substance. The equation below shows the reaction in which ammonia is formed.

$$N_2 (g) + 3H_2 (g) \rightleftharpoons 2NH_3 (g) + \text{heat}$$

The graph below shows how temperature and pressure affect how much ammonia is produced in the reaction.

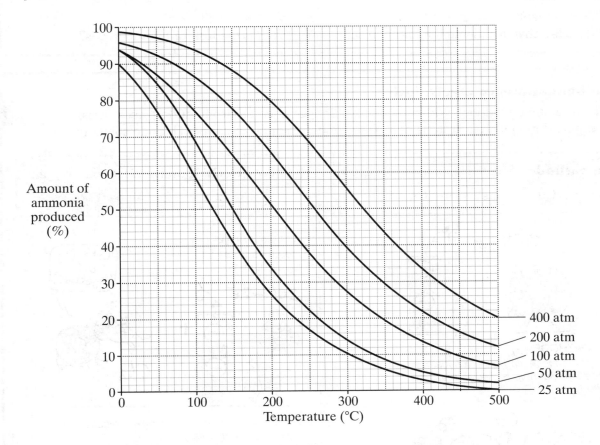

In the industrial process a mixture of nitrogen and hydrogen is passed over iron at a temperature of about 450°C and 200 atmospheres pressure.

(a) Use the graph to find the percentage of ammonia present when the temperature and pressure are 450°C and 200 atmospheres.

....% *(1 mark)*

(b) Explain why the nitrogen and hydrogen mixture is passed over iron.

....

.... *(2 marks)*

H (c) Explain, as fully as you can, using the graph and your knowledge of the Haber process why 450°C and 200 atmospheres were chosen as conditions for this process.

....

....

....

....

....

.... *(8 marks)*

11
marks

Electrolysis

▶ **ThinkAbout:**

1. Which elements make up lead bromide?
2. What is the chemical name for common salt?
3. What is brine?
4. What is the test for hydrogen gas?

▶ **Half-equations in electrolysis**

We can write half-equations to describe the reactions at each electrode during electrolysis. For example, during the electrolysis of molten copper chloride or copper chloride solution:

H

At the **cathode** (negative electrode) we get:

$$Cu^{2+} + 2e^- \longrightarrow Cu$$

At the **anode** (positive electrode) we get:

$$2Cl^- - 2e^- \longrightarrow Cl_2$$

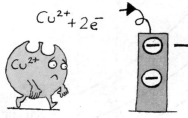

AT THE CATHODE (−)
The copper ion is feeling blue. It's lost two electrons. But help is available at the cathode.

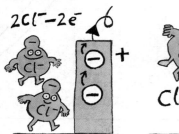

AT THE ANODE (+)
electrons go back to the battery

Let's fly off together.

Two Cl⁻ ions each lose their extra electron and make a Cl₂ molecule

Copper's in the pink. It gets two electrons and changes from an ion to an atom.

Electrolysis is the breakdown of substances containing ions by electricity. It only happens if the ionic compound is molten or dissolved in water ie. when the ions are free to move around.

▶ **Reduction and oxidation**

Positively charged ions are **reduced** at the cathode (−). They *gain* electrons.

At the anode (+), negatively charged ions lose their extra electrons:

Negatively charged ions are **oxidised** at the anode. They *lose* electrons.

▶ **Electrolysis in solutions**

When we electrolyse a solution, we have to take into account water molecules.

At the cathode (−): If the metal in solution is reactive, we get hydrogen gas given off from the water.

At the anode (+): Look at the list opposite. When OH⁻ is discharged, we get oxygen gas given off.

Order of discharge

carbonate, CO_3^{2-}	these ions stay
nitrate, NO_3^-	in solution;
sulfate, SO_4^{2-}	oxygen is given off
hydroxide, OH⁻	ions from water
chloride, Cl⁻	OH⁻ stays in solution;
bromide, Br⁻	the halogen is
iodide, I⁻	given off

Answers: 1. lead and bromine 2. sodium chloride 3. sodium chloride solution 4. a lighted splint pops

▷ Sodium chloride – common salt

We find sodium chloride naturally in the sea and underground as rock salt. It can be pumped up from underground as **brine** (salt solution).

> The brine is electrolysed in industry to form **hydrogen, chlorine** and **sodium hydroxide** solution.

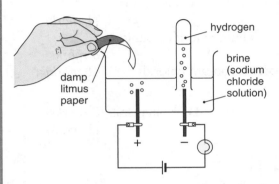

- Hydrogen is given off from the negative electrode.
  (Hydrogen makes a 'pop' – a squeaky explosion – with a lighted splint.)

- Chlorine gas is given off from the positive electrode.
  (Chlorine bleaches damp litmus paper.)

- The solution around the negative electrode turns alkaline (as acidic $H^+(aq)$ ions are removed). This eventually turns the brine into sodium hydroxide solution.

Take care:
- Positive metal ions have to **gain** electrons at the negative electrode in order to change into metal atoms. The ions are **reduced**.

- At the positve electrode, **molecules** of gas often form, such as O_2 or Cl_2, not atoms.

More in **Chemistry for You**, pages 82–89, 92–95, 98–101, 104–106, 108.

▷ Explaining the electrolysis of brine

Look at what happens in the electrolysis of sodium chloride solution:

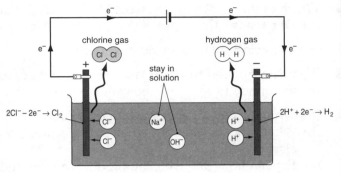

$$2Cl^- - 2e^- \rightarrow Cl_2$$

$$2H^+ + 2e^- \rightarrow H_2$$

▷ Useful products from sodium chloride

Chlorine
- kills bacteria in swimming pools and in drinking water
- manufacture of hydrochloric acid, disinfectant, bleach and PVC

Hydrogen
- making margarine
- manufacture of ammonia to make fertilisers

Sodium hydroxide
- manufacture of paper and ceramics
- making soap, disinfectants and bleach

▷ Purifying copper

Copper is purified by electrolysis.
- The anode (+) is the impure copper.
- The cathode (−) is pure copper.

The copper electrodes dip into a solution containing copper ions.

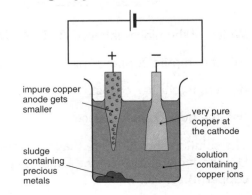

Electrolysis

Homework Questions

1 Which of the following ions would be discharged at the cathode ($-$) during electrolysis?
(a) OH^- (b) Cl^- (c) K^+ (d) Br^- (e) Na^+ (f) SO_4^{2-} (g) H^+ *(2 marks)*

2 At which electrode does oxidation occur?   *(1 mark)*

3 If you electrolysed **molten** lead bromide, what product would you get at:
(a) the anode ($+$)?   (b) the cathode ($-$)?   *(2 marks)*

4 (a) What ions are in sodium chloride solution?   *(1 mark)*
(b) What products are formed at each electrode when sodium chloride solution is electrolysed?   *(1 mark)*
(c) Explain how, and why, the products are formed when sodium chloride solution is electrolysed.   *(3 marks)*
(d) How would the products differ if the electrolyte is **molten** sodium chloride?   *(1 mark)*

5 (a) Which of these would make good electrolytes?
   A pure water   **B** magnesium chloride solution   **C** ethanol   **D** molten salt *(2 marks)*
(b) Explain your answer to part (a).   *(1 mark)*

⊞ **6** Copy and complete these electron half-equations:
(a) $K^+ + e^- \longrightarrow$ ....   (b) $2Br^-$ .... $\longrightarrow Br_2$
(c) Mg^{2+} .... $\longrightarrow Mg$ (d) $4OH^- - 4e^- \longrightarrow 2H_2O +$ ....   *(4 marks)*

⊞ **7** Write the half-equations which occur at each electrode when impure copper is purified by electrolysis.   *(2 marks)* $\overline{20}$ marks

Examination Questions

1 Copper is extracted from the ore called copper pyrites.

(a) The diagram shows a method for changing impure copper into pure copper.

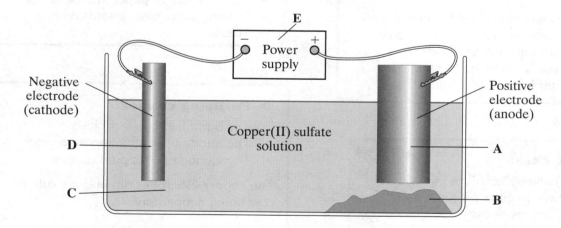

Which of the places labelled **A**, **B**, **C**, **D** or **E** is where:

(i)   the impure copper is placed;   ....

(ii) the impurities collect;   ....

(iii) the pure copper collects?   ....   *(3 marks)*

(b) The solution shown in the diagram contains copper(II) sulfate.
Use the table of ions on the Data Sheet (page 117) to work out the formula of copper(II) sulfate.

The formula of copper(II) sulfate is ....   *(1 mark)* $\overline{4}$ marks

2 Chlorine, hydrogen and sodium hydroxide are produced by the electrolysis of sodium chloride solution.

A student passed electricity through sodium chloride solution using the apparatus shown in the diagram.

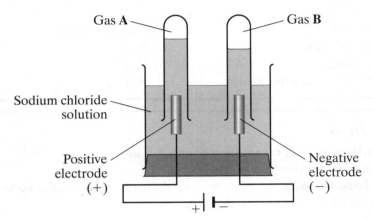

(a) Name:

Gas **A** ....

Gas **B** .... *(1 mark)*

(b) Describe and give the result of a test you could do in a school laboratory to find out which gas is chlorine.

Test ....

....

Result (what you would see) ....

.... *(2 marks)*

(c) (i) Balance the half-equation for the production of hydrogen at one electrode.

.... H$^+$ + ... e^- ⟶ H$_2$ *(1 mark)*

(ii) Which word, from the list, best describes the reaction in part (c)(i)?
Put a ring around the correct word.

decomposition   cracking   neutralisation   oxidation   reduction

(1 mark)

(iii) Name two substances manufactured from hydrogen.

1. ....

2. ....

(2 marks)

(d) Name the substance left in solution at the end.

.... *(1 mark)*

(Note that part (c) (i) is a [H] question.)

8 marks

Answers on page 114

Acids, alkalis and salts

▶ **ThinkAbout:**

1. Name the salt formed when these react:
   a) sodium hydroxide and dilute nitric acid
   b) magnesium and dilute sulfuric acid
   c) copper oxide and dil. hydrochloric acid.

2. Name these salts:
   a) $ZnCl_2$
   b) $Cu(NO_3)_2$
   c) K_2SO_4

▶ **Neutralisation**

We can **neutralise** an acid by reacting it with a base.
Alkalis are bases that can dissolve in water.
Acids form **hydrogen ions**, $H^+(aq)$, and alkalis form **hydroxide ions**, $OH^-(aq)$.
The general equation for a neutralisation reaction is:

acid + a base (or alkali) $\longrightarrow$ a salt + water

For example,

hydrochloric acid + sodium hydroxide $\longrightarrow$ sodium chloride + water
$HCl\ (aq)$ + $NaOH\ (aq)$ $\longrightarrow$ $NaCl\ (aq)$ + $H_2O\ (l)$

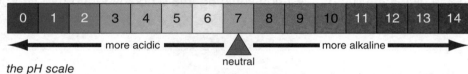

0	1	2	3	4	5	6	7	8	9	10	11	12	13	14

$\longleftarrow$ more acidic ———— neutral ———— more alkaline $\longrightarrow$

the pH scale

▶ **Ionic equations**

We can summarise what happens when an acid and alkali neutralise each other by an ionic equation:

$H^+\ (aq) + OH^-\ (aq) \longrightarrow H_2O\ (l)$

An ionic equation only shows the ions that change in the reaction.

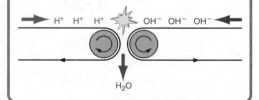

H$^+$ H$^+$ H$^+$ ⚡ OH$^-$ OH$^-$ OH$^-$

H$_2$O

▶ **Salts**

The salt made when we neutralise an acid depends on:
- the acid used, and
- the metal in the base or alkali.

The salt gets the first part of its name from the metal. The last part of its name comes from the acid.

Hydrochloric acid (HCl) makes salts called **chlorides**.
Nitric acid (HNO_3) makes salts called **nitrates**.
Sulfuric acid (H_2SO_4) makes salts called **sulfates**.

Eg. **zinc nitrate**
metal   from acid

When we replace some or all of the hydrogen in an acid by a metal, we get a salt

Answers:

▶ Preparing salts

We can make crystals of salts from acids.

With an insoluble base, such as a transition metal oxide or hydroxide (such as copper oxide), we can filter off the excess base after the acid has been neutralised.

Then we evaporate off some of the water from the salt solution and leave it long enough for the crystals to form.

With an alkali we have to use an indicator to see when the reaction is complete.

Take care:
Most of the salts you meet will start their names with a metal. However, salts formed from the weak alkali, ammonia (NH_3) form **ammonium salts**. Examples are ammonium nitrate (NH_4NO_3) and ammonium sulfate (($NH_4)_2SO_4$). Ammonium salts are important fertilisers.

▶ Reactions that produce salts

We get salts formed in reactions with acids.
Here are some examples of reactions that produce salts:

Acid and metal

$$\text{acid} + \text{a metal} \longrightarrow \text{a salt} + \text{hydrogen}$$
$$H_2SO_4 \text{ (aq)} + Mg \text{ (s)} \longrightarrow MgSO_4 \text{ (aq)} + H_2 \text{ (g)}$$

Here is magnesium reacting with dilute sulfuric acid. The excess magnesium will be removed by filtering before crystallising out the magnesium sulfate.

- This method is for metals that are **more reactive** than hydrogen. It will not work with metals, such as copper, that can't displace hydrogen from the acidic solution.
- This method should not be used with highly reactive metals, such as sodium or potassium, because the reaction is too violent and will explode.

Acid and base

$$\text{acid} + \text{a base (insoluble)} \longrightarrow \text{a salt} + \text{water}$$
$$H_2SO_4 \text{ (aq)} + CuO \text{ (s)} \longrightarrow CuSO_4 \text{ (aq)} + H_2O \text{ (l)}$$

Acid and alkali

$$\text{acid} + \text{an alkali (a soluble base)} \longrightarrow \text{a salt} + \text{water}$$
$$HNO_3 \text{ (aq)} + KOH \text{ (aq)} \longrightarrow KNO_3 \text{ (aq)} + H_2O \text{ (l)}$$

See titration on page 89 for a suitable method to prepare the salt.

Precipitation reactions

This method is used when the salt you want to make is insoluble in water, eg.

$$\text{barium chloride} + \text{sodium sulfate} \longrightarrow \text{barium sulfate (the precipitate)} + \text{sodium chloride}$$
$$BaCl_2 \text{ (aq)} + Na_2SO_4 \text{ (aq)} \longrightarrow BaSO_4 \text{ (s)} + 2\,NaCl \text{ (aq)}$$

- The precipitate formed is washed with distilled water and then dried to leave pure insoluble salt.

- Precipitation reactions are used to help purify drinking water and to treat waste-water (effluent).

More in *Chemistry for You,* pages 124–129, 132–133, 136–138.

Acids, alkalis and salts

Homework Questions

1 Explain the difference between an alkali and a base. Give one example of each.   *(3 marks)*

2 If you spilled some dilute sodium hydroxide solution on your desk, it could be neutralised with:
(a) vinegar   (b) toothpaste   (c) limewater   (d) sodium carbonate solution. *(1 mark)*

3 If you were stung by a wasp, you could reduce the pain by rubbing the area of your skin with vinegar. What does this tell you about the wasp sting?   *(1 mark)*

4 Copy and complete these equations for some neutralisation reactions:
(a) $HNO_3 + KOH \longrightarrow$ .... + ...   *(1 mark)*
(b) .... + ... $\longrightarrow 2NaCl + H_2O + CO_2$ *(1 mark)*

5 In this equation, $H_2SO_4 + 2NaOH \longrightarrow Na_2SO_4 + 2H_2O$
what are the symbols for the ions responsible for neutralisation?   *(2 marks)*

6 Which salt is made from the reaction between:
(a) sulfuric acid and potassium hydroxide?   *(1 mark)*
(b) nitric acid and copper(II) oxide?   *(1 mark)*

7 When making salts:
(a) why do we need an indicator if NaOH is used, but not if $Cu(OH)_2$ is used?   *(1 mark)*
(b) when would you use a titration method?   *(1 mark)*
(c) when would you use a precipitation method?   *(1 mark)*   **15**
(d) why do we sometimes evaporate some of the water from a salt solution?   *(1 mark)* marks

Examination Questions

1 (a) Which acid from the list should the student add to sodium hydroxide solution to make sodium sulfate?

    ethanoic acid   **hydrochloric acid**   **nitric acid**   **sulfuric acid**   *(1 mark)*

  (b) When the acid was added to the alkali the beaker became warm.
     Name the type of reaction that releases heat.

     .... *(1 mark)*

  (c) Use the Data Sheet (on page 117) to help you to write the formula of sodium sulfate.

     Formula: .... *(1 mark)*

  (d) (i) Name the gas given off when zinc reacts with hydrochloric acid.

       .... *(1 mark)*

    (ii) How would you positively identify this gas?

       .... *(1 mark)*

    (iii) Name the salt formed in the reaction.   **6**

     .... *(1 mark)* marks

2 Neutralisation reactions can be used to make salts.

(a) Write an ionic equation for a neutralisation reaction, including state symbols.

.... *(1 mark)*

(b) Ammonium nitrate is a salt used as a fertiliser.

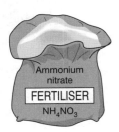

Ammonium nitrate is made by mixing two solutions. Name these solutions.

.... and .... *(2 marks)*

$\overline{\quad 3 \quad}$
marks

3 When a solution of lead nitrate is added to a solution of sodium chloride, a white precipitate of lead chloride is produced.

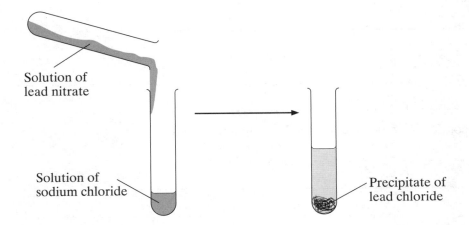

(a) (i) Why is a precipitate formed?

....

.... *(1 mark)*

(ii) Complete and balance the equation for this precipitation reaction:

$$Pb^{+2}\ (aq) + Cl^-\ (aq) \longrightarrow \qquad\qquad \text{\textit{(2 marks)}}$$

(b) Complete the table below by writing in the name and formula of the precipitate formed for each reaction. If there is no precipitate, write 'no precipitate'.

Solution 1	Added to	Solution 2	Name of precipitate formed	Formula
(i) copper sulfate	→	sodium hydroxide		
(ii) lead nitrate	→	magnesium sulfate		
(iii) sodium chloride	→	zinc nitrate		

(5 marks)

$\overline{\quad 8 \quad}$
marks

Answers on page 114

Getting the Grades – Structures and bonding

Try this question, then compare your answer with the two examples opposite ▶

The diagram shows the arrangement of ions in a crystal of sodium chloride.

(a) (i) Describe how sodium and chlorine atoms change into sodium and chloride ions.

Cl⁻ ion

Na⁺ ion

....

....

....

.... *(2 marks)*

(ii) Which group in the Periodic Table contains elements with the same electronic structures as sodium and chloride ions?

.... *(1 mark)*

(b) Describe and explain the following properties of sodium chloride:

(i) melting point

....

....

....

.... *(3 marks)*

(ii) ability to conduct electricity when solid and when molten

....

....

....

.... *(2 marks)*

(c) The structural formula of a hydrazine molecule is shown opposite.

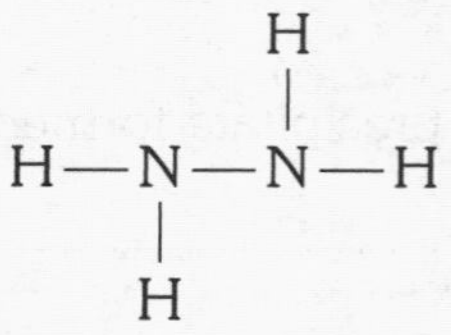

$$H-\overset{\displaystyle H}{\underset{\displaystyle H}{N}}-\overset{}{\underset{\displaystyle H}{N}}-H$$

(i) Complete the diagram below to show how the outer energy level (shell) electrons are arranged in a hydrazine molecule. Show the electrons as dots and crosses.

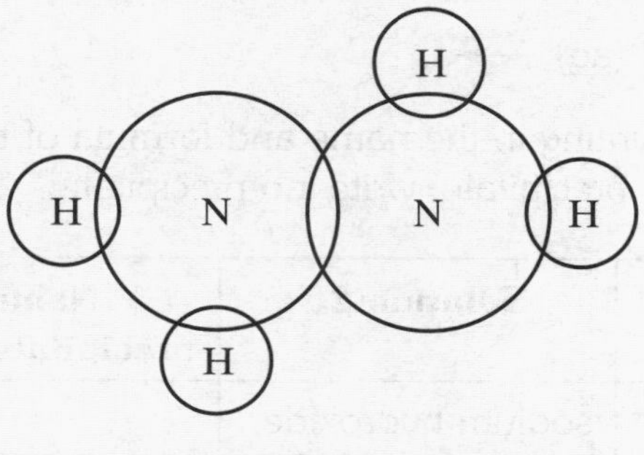

H   N   N   H

H

H

(2 marks)

H (ii) Explain why hydrazine has a low boiling point.

....

.... *(2 marks)*

12 marks

80

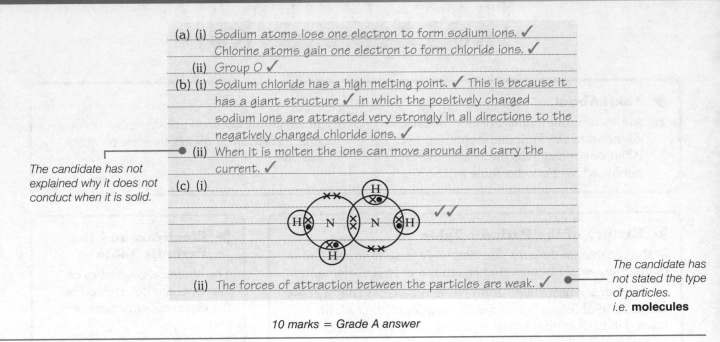

(a) (i) Sodium atoms lose one electron to form sodium ions. ✓
        Chlorine atoms gain one electron to form chloride ions. ✓
    (ii) Group O ✓
(b) (i) Sodium chloride has a high melting point. ✓ This is because it
        has a giant structure ✓ in which the positively charged
        sodium ions are attracted very strongly in all directions to the
        negatively charged chloride ions. ✓
    (ii) When it is molten the ions can move around and carry the
         current. ✓
(c) (i)

The candidate has not explained why it does not conduct when it is solid.

✓✓

(ii) The forces of attraction between the particles are weak. ✓

The candidate has not stated the type of particles.
i.e. molecules

10 marks = Grade A answer

▶ **Improve your Grades   A up to A***

Remember that ionic compounds have giant structures.
Grade A* candidates are expected to apply their knowledge to unfamiliar situations. The arrangement of electrons in a hydrazine molecule is not in the specification but you should be able to work it out using the structural formula given in the question. Remember each of the lines between atoms in the structural formula represents a covalent bond which is a shared pair of electrons.

GRADE 'C' ANSWER

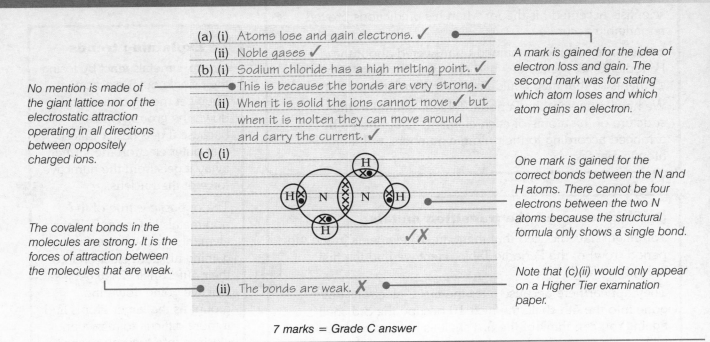

(a) (i) Atoms lose and gain electrons. ✓
    (ii) Noble gases ✓
(b) (i) Sodium chloride has a high melting point. ✓
        This is because the bonds are very strong. ✓
    (ii) When it is solid the ions cannot move ✓ but
         when it is molten they can move around
         and carry the current. ✓
(c) (i)

No mention is made of the giant lattice nor of the electrostatic attraction operating in all directions between oppositely charged ions.

A mark is gained for the idea of electron loss and gain. The second mark was for stating which atom loses and which atom gains an electron.

One mark is gained for the correct bonds between the N and H atoms. There cannot be four electrons between the two N atoms because the structural formula only shows a single bond.

The covalent bonds in the molecules are strong. It is the forces of attraction between the molecules that are weak.

✓✗

(ii) The bonds are weak. ✗

Note that (c)(ii) would only appear on a Higher Tier examination paper.

7 marks = Grade C answer

▶ **Improve your Grades   C up to B**

Remember that giant structures have high melting points and boiling points.
Substances which are made of small molecules have low melting points and boiling points.
Metals reacting with non-metals produce ionic compounds.
Non-metals reacting with non-metals produce covalent compounds.

The Periodic Table

▶ ThinkAbout:

1. Are there more metallic or non-metallic elements in the Periodic Table?
2. What nationality was the chemist who published his Periodic Table in 1869?
3. In which part of the Periodic Table do you find the group of metals that are most reactive?

▶ History of the Periodic Table

In the nineteenth century chemists were busy trying to find the fundamental patterns that linked the chemical elements.

An English scientist called John Newlands had a little success when he tried listing the elements in order of their atomic mass. He noticed that *every eighth element was similar.* Unfortunately, the pattern broke down after the first 15 of the elements known at that time.

However, he was on the right lines. In 1869 a Russian chemist, called Dmitri Mendeleev, solved the problem. He left gaps in his table of elements so that similar elements always lined up in columns. He argued that the gaps would be filled when new elements were discovered.

He even predicted the properties of missing elements from the patterns he could see in his Periodic Table. Other scientists accepted his theory when his predictions proved remarkably accurate.

Some strange things remained unanswered about the Periodic Table. Mendeleev had changed the order of a few elements so that they could line up in their groups, but why?

We now know that the Periodic Table is related to the structure of the atoms of each element. They should be arranged according to their atomic numbers, not their atomic masses.

▶ Electrons and the transition metals

You might have noticed that there are 18 elements in the 4th period (row) of the Periodic Table. Here we find the first transition metals.

H

They appear here because after the first 2 electrons have gone into the 4th shell, the next 10 occupy the 3rd shell again. You can think of the 3rd shell as holding 8 electrons, with 10 'in reserve'. These electrons account for the special properties of the transition metals. (See next page.)

▶ Electrons and the Periodic Table

The chemical properties of elements are determined by the electronic structures of their atoms.

The number of electrons in the **outer shell** (or highest energy level) is important.

> The atoms of elements in the same group have the same number of electrons in their outer shell.

▶ Explaining trends

Group 1 metals react by losing their single outer electron. They get more reactive going down the group. That's because it gets easier to lose that outer electron the further away it gets from the attractive force of the nucleus.

H

The opposite is true of the non-metals in Group 7. Their elements react with metals by gaining an extra electron into their outer shell. They get less reactive going down the group, as the larger atoms find it more difficult to attract an electron into their outer shell. That is because the incoming electron is further away from the attractive force of the positively charged nucleus.

Group numbers	1	2											H 1 hydrogen			3	4	5	6	7	0 He 2 helium
	Li 3 lithium	Be 4 beryllium													B 5 boron	C 6 carbon	N 7 nitrogen	O 8 oxygen	F 9 fluorine	Ne 10 neon
	Na 11 sodium	Mg 12 magnesium													Al 13 aluminium	Si 14 silicon	P 15 phosphorus	S 16 sulphur	Cl 17 chlorine	Ar 18 argon
	K 19 potassium	Ca 20 calcium	Sc 21 scandium	Ti 22 titanium	V 23 vanadium	Cr 24 chromium	Mn 25 manganese	Fe 26 iron	Co 27 cobalt	Ni 28 nickel	Cu 29 copper	Zn 30 zinc			Ga 31 gallium	Ge 32 germanium	As 33 arsenic	Se 34 selenium	Br 35 bromine	Kr 36 krypton
	Rb 37 rubidium	Sr 38 strontium	Y 39 yttrium	Zr 40 zirconium	Nb 41 niobium	Mo 42 molybdenum	Tc 43 technetium	Ru 44 ruthenium	Rh 45 rhodium	Pd 46 palladium	Ag 47 silver	Cd 48 cadmium			In 49 indium	Sn 50 tin	Sb 51 antimony	Te 52 tellurium	I 53 iodine	Xe 54 xenon
	Cs 55 caesium	Ba 56 barium	La 57 lanthanum	Hf 72 hafnium	Ta 73 tantalum	W 74 tungsten	Re 75 rhenium	Os 76 osmium	Ir 77 iridium	Pt 78 platinum	Au 79 gold	Hg 80 mercury			Tl 81 thallium	Pb 82 lead	Bi 83 bismuth	Po 84 polonium	At 85 astatine	Rn 86 radon

▶ **Group 1** elements are the metals called the **alkali metals**.

- For metals, they have low densities and are soft.
- They are very reactive metals.
- They get more reactive as we go down the group.
- Their melting points and boiling points decrease going down the group.
- Most of the compounds of alkali metals are white and are soluble in water.
- They react with non-metals to produce ionic compounds, forming ions with a 1+ charge.
- When dropped onto water, they fizz around the surface, giving off hydrogen gas and forming an alkaline solution of the metal hydroxide.
  Eg.

  sodium + water ⟶ sodium hydroxide + hydrogen

  $2Na\,(s) + 2H_2O\,(l) \longrightarrow 2NaOH\,(aq) + H_2\,(g)$

▶ **Group 7** elements are the non-metals called the **halogens**.

- They react with metals to produce ionic salts, forming ions with a 1− charge.
- They react with other non-metals to form molecules, in which the atoms are joined by covalent bonds.
- They all have coloured vapours and exist as diatomic molecules, for example, Br_2.
- They become less reactive going down the group. So a more reactive halogen can **displace** a less reactive halogen from a solution of its halide salt.
  Eg.
  bromine + sodium iodide
  ⟶ sodium bromide + iodine
- Their melting points and boiling points increase going down the group.

▶ **The transition metals** – found between Groups 2 and 3

- The transition metals are hard, strong, dense and have high melting points (except mercury).
- They are **not very reactive**.
- They form **coloured compounds**.

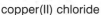
copper(II) chloride

nickel chloride

iron(III) chloride

- They form ions with **different charges**, eg. Fe^{2+} and Fe^{3+}.
- The transition metals are also important **catalysts** in industry.

Groups are families of elements. The members of the family are similar but not exactly the same.

More in **Chemistry for You**, pages 39–55, 60–62.

The Periodic Table

Homework Questions

1 (a) Which scientist first arranged the elements in order of their atomic masses? *(1 mark)*
  (b) Which scientist left gaps in his version of the Periodic Table, for elements yet to be
     discovered? *(1 mark)*

2 The boxes in the Periodic Table have numbers and symbols for the elements.
   What do the numbers tell you? *(1 mark)*

3 What is the 'family' name for those elements which include copper, nickel and iron? *(1 mark)*

4 What do the elements in Group 1 have in common, in terms of their electrons? *(1 mark)*

5 What do the elements in Group 7 have in common, in terms of their electrons? *(1 mark)*

6 Which is the most reactive element in (a) Group 1, (b) Group 7? *(2 marks)*

7 Why are the Group 1 elements called 'the alkali metals'? *(1 mark)*

8 Which of the following is **not** true about alkali metals?
   A They have low melting points.
   B They are reactive metals.
   C They are soft metals.
   D They mostly form coloured compounds. *(1 mark)*

9 (a) What is the symbol for an iodide ion? *(1 mark)*
   (b) What is the type of bond between a metal and a halogen? *(1 mark)*
   (c) What is formed when you bubble chlorine thorough a solution of sodium
      bromide? *(1 mark)*

10 Why have transition metal compounds long been used in decorating plates and vases? *(1 mark)*

14 marks

Examination Questions

1 This question is about a part of the Periodic Table.
   Choose words from the list for each of the labels **1–4** in the table. Use **each** answer **once**
   only.

   an alkali metal

   a noble gas

   a transition metal used in the form of steel

   a transition metal that weathers to a green colour

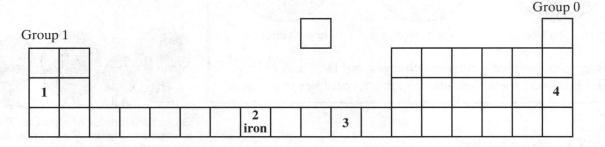

(4 marks) 4 marks

2 The elements in Mendeleev's Periodic Table were arranged in order of increasing atomic mass. Part of the modern Periodic Table is shown.

													H						He
													1						2

Li	Be												B	C	N	O	F	Ne
3	4												5	6	7	8	9	10
Na	Mg												Al	Si	P	S	Cl	Ar
11	12												13	14	15	16	17	18
K	Ca																	
19	20																	

(a) Complete the sentence by writing in the missing words.
The modern Periodic Table is arranged in order of increasing

.... *(1 mark)*

(b) (i) Name a metal from the table above that is in the same group as lithium.

.... *(1 mark)*

(ii) Name a non-metal in the same period as magnesium.

.... *(1 mark)*

(c) The table below contains some information about two elements.

Element	Symbol	Number of		
		protons	neutrons	electrons
fluorine	F	9	10	9
chlorine	Cl	17	18	17
chlorine	Cl	17	20	17

(i) In terms of atomic structure, give **one** feature that both these elements have in common.

.... *(1 mark)*

(ii) There are two **isotopes** of chlorine shown in the table. Explain what **isotope** means.

....

....

.... *(2 marks)*

[H] (iii) Explain, in terms of electron arrangement, why fluorine is more reactive than chlorine.

....

....

.... *(2 marks)*

8 marks

Answers on page 114

More about Acids and Bases

▶ **ThinkAbout:**

1. What do we call a reaction in which the products can re-form the reactants?
2. What is formed when an acid and a base react together?
3. What colour would universal indicator be in a 1 mol/dm^3 solution of sodium hydroxide?

▶ **Ionisation in water**

Acids

For acids to show their acidic properties, water must be present. This is because only when the acids are in solution, can their molecules split up (ionise) to form **H$^+$(aq) ions**. It is these H$^+$ (aq) ions – protons surrounded by water molecules – that give an acidic solution its characteristic properties:

$$HCl \, (g) \xrightarrow{\text{water}} H^+ \, (aq) + Cl^- \, (aq)$$

Whereas excess H$^+$ (aq) ions cause acidity in a solution, an excess of hydroxide ions, **OH$^-$ (aq)**, cause a solution to be alkaline.

- If almost all the acidic molecules in a solution split up (**complete ionisation**), we call the acid a **strong acid**. Examples include hydrochloric acid, nitric acid and sulfuric acid.
- On the other hand, only a few of the molecules of **weak acids**, such as citric acid, ethanoic acid and carbonic acid, split up in a solution.

Therefore given solutions of equal concentration, a strong acid will have a lower pH value than a weak acid. The strong acid will also react faster than a weak acid, for example with magnesium ribbon, because there is a higher concentration of H$^+$(aq) ions in its solution.

Bases

Ammonia is a weak alkali:

$$NH_3 \, (aq) + H_2O \, (l) \rightleftharpoons NH_4^+ \, (aq) + OH^- \, (aq)$$
ammonia   hydroxide ion

We say that ammonia is a weak base or alkali because in its solution there is an equilibrium mixture. There are many undissociated ammonia molecules in its solution. This is like the weak acid we looked at above.

Strong bases or alkalis will ionise (split up into ions) almost completely. Examples of strong alkalis are sodium hydroxide (NaOH) and potassium hydroxide (KOH).

Partial ionisation of a weak acid.
Solutions of weak acids contain 'undissociated' (whole) molecules in equilibrium with H$^+$ ions and negative ions

---

▶ **Definitions**

We can define acids and bases as follows:

| Acids are said to be proton (H$^+$) **donors**, whereas bases are proton **acceptors**. |

H

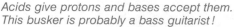

Acids give protons and bases accept them. This busker is probably a bass guitarist!

Answers: 1. reversible reaction   2. a salt plus water   3. purple

▶ Titrations

We can measure the volume of acid and alkali that react together using titration with a suitable indicator.

To signal the end of the reaction, we use an acid–base indicator. When it changes colour we have just the right amount of acid and alkali for a complete reaction. For a strong acid reacting with a strong alkali, any indicator will do.

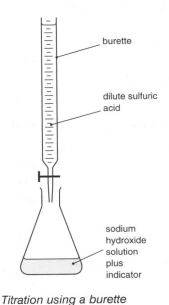

burette

dilute sulfuric acid

sodium hydroxide solution plus indicator

Titration using a burette

More in **Chemistry for You**, pages 130, 226–228, 354–355.

▶ Choosing indicators H

We can measure the volumes of acidic and alkaline solutions that react together using **titration** (see above).

However, not all indicators work well in combinations other than strong acid plus strong alkali.

> For a strong acid plus a weak alkali, use **methyl orange** indicator.
> For a weak acid plus a strong alkali, use **phenolphthalein** indicator.

▶ Titration calculations

- The concentration of a solution is given in moles per dm^3 (mol/dm^3).
- We can work out how many moles are in a **certain** volume of a solution with a known concentration, using this equation:

number of moles in a solution
$$= \text{its concentration} \times \left(\frac{\text{volume of solution in cm}^3}{1000} \right)$$

- We can work out the concentration of **unknown solutions** using the technique of titration.
- The balanced equation tells us the ratio of the **numbers of moles** of reactants involved in the titration reaction. Then we can use the fact that concentrations are expressed in moles per dm^3 (mol/dm^3) to give the answer (which you may have to convert to g/dm^3.)

Example

$10 \ cm^3$ of $0.1 \ mol/dm^3$ hydrochloric acid is neutralised by $20 \ cm^3$ of dilute sodium hydroxide. What is the concentration of the sodium hydroxide solution?

The equation for the neutralisation is:

$$\text{NaOH (aq)} + \text{HCl (aq)} \longrightarrow \text{NaCl (aq)} + \text{H}_2\text{O (l)}$$

- So 1 mole of hydrochloric acid reacts with 1 mole of sodium hydroxide.
- So in $20 \ cm^3$ of the unknown sodium hydroxide solution, there must be the same number of moles as there are in $10 \ cm^3$ of $0.1 \ mol/dm^3$ hydrochloric acid.
- Because we need twice the volume of sodium hydroxide, it must be half the concentration of the acid ie. **$0.05 \ mol/dm^3$**.

▶ More about acids and bases H

A young Swedish chemist called **Svante Arrhenius** was the first to suggest that molecules could split up or dissociate. In 1884 he put forward his ideas in his PhD thesis.

His professors barely passed his work because they could not believe that molecules could split up in water. Svante spent much of his time trying to persuade his fellow chemists that his ideas made sense. Most people finally believed him when the evidence for charged particles in atoms was found in the 1890s. Svante was eventually rewarded with a Nobel Prize in 1903.

Later work on acids and bases by **Brønsted** and **Lowry** extended the ideas of Arrhenius. They said that acids give away H^+ ions (protons) and bases accept H^+ ions. This was more easily accepted as it helped to explain acid behaviour in solvents other than water. The theory was not as revolutionary as Svante's original ideas!

More about acids and bases

Homework Questions

1 Copy and complete these dissociation (ionisation) equations:
(a) $HNO_3 \longrightarrow$ .... + ...
(b) $H_2SO_4 \longrightarrow$ .... + ...   *(4 marks)*

2 Classify these acids as either **strong** acids or **weak** acids:
carbonic, hydrochloric, ethanoic, citric, sulfuric, nitric, tartaric   *(7 marks)*

Ⓗ **3** Why are acids called **proton** donors?   *(1 mark)*

4 If the acids are of equal concentration, which of these acids will react quickest with the same mass of iron filings? **A** carbonic acid **B** ethanoic acid **C** nitric acid **D** tartaric acid *(1 mark)*

5 Which equation for a dissociation (ionisation) reaction will have fewest ions present at equilibrium?
A $NaOH \rightleftharpoons Na^+ + OH^-$ **B** $KOH \rightleftharpoons K^+ + OH^-$
C $NH_3 + H_2O \rightleftharpoons NH_4^+ + OH^-$ **D** $LiOH \rightleftharpoons Li^+ + OH^-$ *(1 mark)*

Ⓗ **6** Which scientist is **not** credited with the development of acid–base theories?
A Priestley   **B** Arrhenius   **C** Lowry   **D** Brønsted   *(1 mark)*

7 Why do chemists often use a burette when carrying out titration reactions?   *(1 mark)*

8 Copy and complete these equations for neutralisation reactions. (CH_3COOH is ethanoic acid.)
(a) $KOH + HNO_3 \longrightarrow$ .... + ...   *(1 mark)*
(b) $NaOH + CH_3COOH \longrightarrow$ .... + ...   *(1 mark)*

Ⓗ **9** 20 cm^3 of 0.2 mol/dm^3 hydrochloric acid is neutralised by 25 cm^3 of dilute sodium hydroxide solution. What is the concentration of the sodium hydroxide solution?   *(1 mark)*

Ⓗ **10** Suggest an appropriate indicator for use in a titration between ethanoic acid and sodium hydroxide solution.   *(1 mark)*

20 marks

Examination Questions

1 The diagrams show what happens when an acid is added to an alkali.

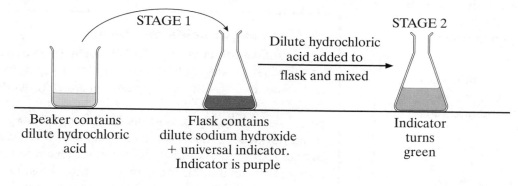

STAGE 1   STAGE 2

Dilute hydrochloric acid added to flask and mixed

Beaker contains dilute hydrochloric acid

Flask contains dilute sodium hydroxide + universal indicator. Indicator is purple

Indicator turns green

(a) What is in the flask at stage 2, besides universal indicator and water?

.... *(1 mark)*

(b) Write an ionic equation to show how water is formed in this reaction and state the sources of the ions.

....

....

.... *(3 marks)*

4 marks

2 (a) The reaction on mixing solutions of sodium hydroxide and hydrochloric acid is shown.

$$NaOH + HCl \longrightarrow NaCl + H_2O$$

Write the balanced ionic equation for this reaction.

.... *(2 marks)*

(b) Varying amounts of sodium hydroxide solution and hydrochloric acid were mixed, but the total volume of the mixture was always 50 cm³. The temperatures of the solutions before and after mixing were recorded. A graph of the results is shown.

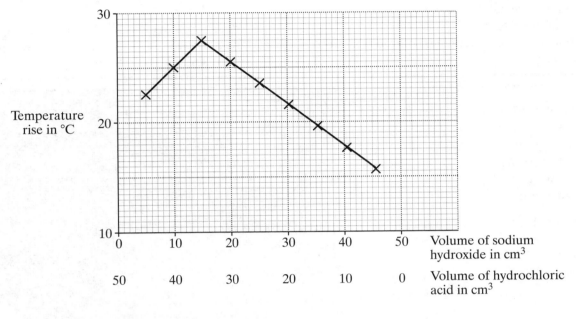

(i) What was the highest temperature rise?

.... *(1 mark)*

(ii) Explain how the highest temperature rise shows that the sodium hydroxide solution has a higher concentration than the hydrochloric acid solution.

....

....

....

....

.... *(3 marks)*

H (c) Calculate the concentration in mol/dm³ of a solution that was made by dissolving 100 g of sodium hydroxide and making the solution up to 1.0 dm³.
(Relative atomic masses: H = 1; O = 16; Na = 23)

....

....

....

....

....

Concentration of sodium hydroxide solution = ... mol/dm³   9
(3 marks) marks

Answers on page 115

▶ **ThinkAbout:**

1. What is the source of the energy that drives the water cycle?
2. What do we call the type of water that forms a scum with soap?
3. What is the main source of nitrate pollution in water?

4. Which statement is true:
   A Most solids get more soluble in water as the temperature rises, but most gases get less soluble.
   B Most solids get less soluble in water as the temperature rises, but most gases get more soluble.

▶ **The water cycle**

Water is a good **solvent**. It forms **solutions** with many **solutes**.

The 'water cycle' shows how water moves around the Earth.

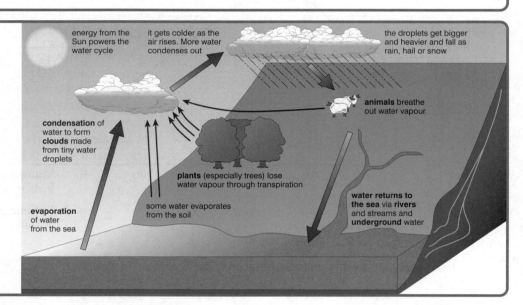

energy from the Sun powers the water cycle

it gets colder as the air rises. More water condenses out

the droplets get bigger and heavier and fall as rain, hail or snow

animals breathe out water vapour

condensation of water to form **clouds** made from tiny water droplets

plants (especially trees) lose water vapour through transpiration

water **returns to the sea** via **rivers** and streams and **underground** water

evaporation of water from the sea

some water evaporates from the soil

▶ **Hard water**

Drinking water is purified by **physical** means (filter beds of sand and gravel to remove solids) and **chemical** means (chlorine to kill bacteria) before it reaches our taps.

> **Hard water** contains dissolved **calcium** ions (Ca^{2+} (aq)) and/or **magnesium** ions (Mg^{2+} (aq)).

We can soften the water by **precipitating** these ions out of solution:

calcium ions (aq)   +   sodium carbonate (aq)

↓

calcium carbonate (s)   +   sodium ions (aq)

Or we can soften hard water by passing it through an **ion exchange column**. Look at the diagram opposite:

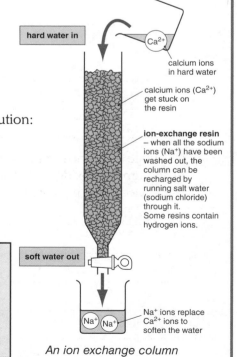

hard water in

Ca^{2+}

calcium ions in hard water

calcium ions (Ca^{2+}) get stuck on the resin

ion-exchange resin – when all the sodium ions (Na^+) have been washed out, the column can be recharged by running salt water (sodium chloride) through it. Some resins contain hydrogen ions.

soft water out

Na^+ Na^+

Na^+ ions replace Ca^{2+} ions to soften the water

An ion exchange column

Disadvantages of hard water	Advantages of hard water
Difficult to form lather with soap.	Some people prefer the taste.
Scum forms in a reaction which wastes soap.	Calcium in the water is good for children's teeth and bones.
Scale (a hard crust) forms inside kettles. This wastes energy when you boil your kettle.	Helps to reduce heart illness.
	Some brewers like hard water for making beer.
Hot water pipes 'fur up' on the inside. The scale formed can even block up pipes completely.	A coating of scale (limescale) inside copper or lead pipes stops poisonous salts dissolving into our water.

Answers: 4. A   3. nitrate fertilisers   2. hard water   1. the Sun

▶ Water pollution

Water is used as a **coolant** in industry. For example, it takes heat energy away from exothermic reactions in the Contact process used to manufacture sulfuric acid. It also transfers heat in power stations. If hot water that has been used as a coolant is pumped out into rivers it causes **thermal pollution** of the habitat. The delicate balance of nature is disturbed and aquatic life suffers. For example, the hotter the water, the less oxygen gas dissolves in it.

I take no chances with thermal pollution nowadays!

▶ Water fit to drink

Here is a flow chart of what happens to water before it gets to your taps at home:

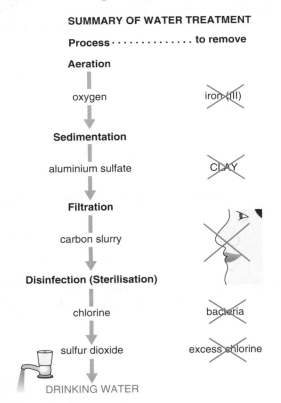

SUMMARY OF WATER TREATMENT

Process · · · · · · · · · · · · · **to remove**

Aeration

oxygen — iron (III)

Sedimentation

aluminium sulfate — CLAY

Filtration

carbon slurry

Disinfection (Sterilisation)

chlorine — bacteria

sulfur dioxide — excess chlorine

DRINKING WATER

More in *Chemistry for You*, pages 284, 288–300, 305.

▶ Solubility curves

Unlike gases, the solubility of most solids increases as we raise the temperature. We can show this on solubility curves:

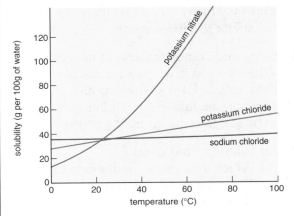

Notice that we measure solubility in grams of solute per 100 grams of water at any given temperature.

A **saturated solution** is one in which no more solute will dissolve at that temperature. If you cool a saturated solution the solute crystallises out.

▶ Fizzy drinks

The solubility of a gas increases with increasing pressure. You see this when you open a can of fizzy drink. The pressure is lowered and the dissolved carbon dioxide escapes.

▶ Distilling

In some countries they have to convert sea-water into useable water. They do this in a process called desalination. One way to do this involves distilling the salty water. This is an expensive process because of the energy involved in heating the salt solution.

▶ Water filters

Some people pass the water they intend to drink through water filters.
These filters can contain:
- carbon (to remove unwanted tastes and smells
- silver (to kill bacteria)
- ion exchange resins (to remove metal ions, eg. calcium and magnesium ions that cause hardness, as well as toxic heavy metal pollutants).

Aqueous chemistry

Homework Questions

1 Explain what we mean by the terms:
(a) solute   (b) solvent   (c) solution.   *(3 marks)*

2 Copy and complete these sentences:
When the sea is warmed, some of the water .... into the sky. As the water vapour
rises, clouds form as the vapour .... When the droplets are large enough, ... ,
snow or hail falls. Some of this gets .... by plant roots, and passes through the plant
to be lost into the air by the process of ....   *(5 marks)*

3 (a) What is 'hard water'?   *(1 mark)*
(b) Which ions cause hardness in water?   *(2 marks)*
(c) There are good points and bad points in using hard water. Give **three** advantages and
    three disadvantages of using hard water.   *(6 marks)*

4 Explain what we mean by thermal pollution of water, and state one of the consequences for
the animals that live in the water.   *(2 marks)*

5 Explain the processes of sedimentation, filtration, and chlorination in water
purification.   *(3 marks)*

6 What would you expect to see when a saturated solution cools down?   *(1 mark)*

7 Where in the world would you see lots of desalination plants used for water
purification?   *(1 mark)*

8 Which of the three substances shown in the graph on page 93 is the most soluble
at 10°C?   *(1 mark)*

25
marks

Examination Questions

1 (a) A sample of natural hard water contains these ions:

calcium   chloride   hydrogencarbonate   magnesium   sodium   sulfate

Which two ions make the water hard?

1. ....   2. .... *(2 marks)*

(b) A sample of hard water was shaken with ten drops of soap solution. Scum was formed
   but no lather. An equal volume of hard water was boiled then shaken with 10 drops of
   soap solution. A lather was formed.

   (i) Why did the boiled water form a lather?

   ....

   .... *(1 mark)*

   (ii) A sample of hard water was passed through an ion exchange column. What would
       you see when the treated water was shaken with soap solution?

   .... *(1 mark)*

4
marks

2 Water from rivers has to be treated before we can drink it.

(a) Why is the water passed through filter beds?

.... (1 mark)

(b) Why is chlorine added to the water?

.... (1 mark)

(c) Some people also use water filters at home before drinking tap water.
Match the substances contained in these filters to the reason they are used.

Substance in filter	**Why it is used**
A Ion exchange resin	1. kills bacteria
B carbon	2. removes metal ions
C silver	3. removes substances that cause nasty tastes and smells

(2 marks)

4 marks

3 Some substances dissolve in water.
The solubility of a substance is the number of grams that will dissolve in 100 grams of water.
The diagram below shows how the solubilities of two substances, potassium nitrate and sodium chloride, vary between 0°C and 100°C.

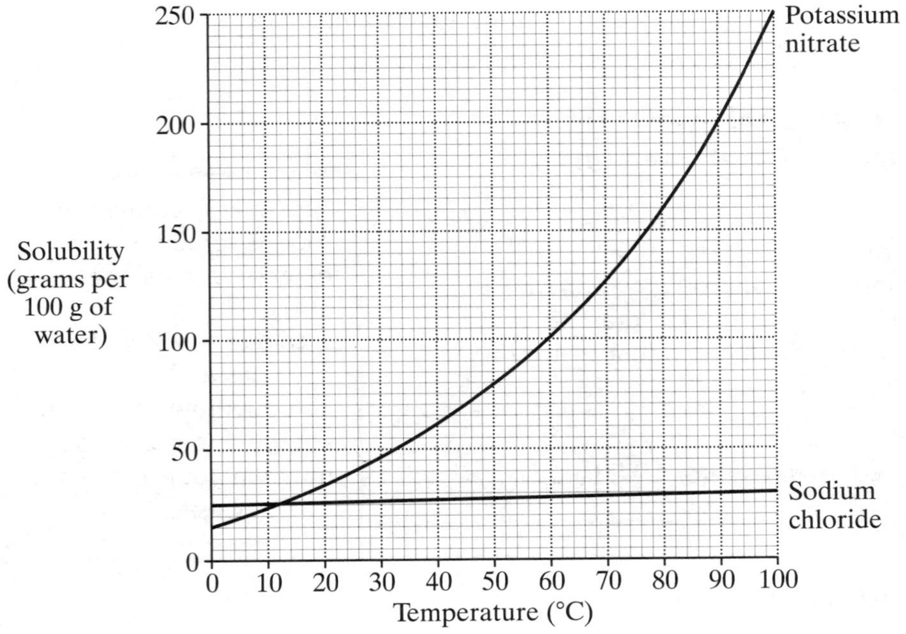

(a) How much potassium nitrate dissolves in 100 grams of water at 60°C? .... grams
(1 mark)

(b) Describe what happens to the solubilities of potassium nitrate and sodium chloride between 0°C and 100°C. Answer in as much detail as you can.

....

....

....

....

....
(5 marks)

6 marks

Energy

▶ **ThinkAbout:**

1. You add a solid to a solution in a boiling tube and the substances react. The bottom of the tube feels really cold. Why?

2. Do you think we need to put energy into a compound to break its bonds, or do you think energy will be given out in this process?

▶ **Comparing fuels**

One of the main factors to think about when choosing a fuel is its energy content. To compare this across different fuels we should look at the energy released per gram of fuel burned.

To get this information by experiment, you need to carry out a fair test. The only variable that should change each time we collect data is the type of fuel.

To make the investigation valid we want the energy released as the fuel burns to heat up the water. Therefore we use a copper beaker (called a calorimeter).

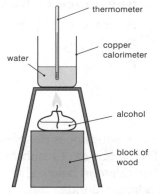

Apparatus for comparing fuels

You will also need to weigh how much fuel is used in each test.

Then you can work out how much energy (in joules) is transferred to the water.

To convert this energy into the amount of energy per gram, we use this equation:

$$\text{Energy per gram} = \frac{\text{energy released (J)}}{\text{mass of fuel used (g)}}$$

Example 1

0.2 g of fuel raised the temperature of 100 g of water by 5°C. How much energy does the fuel give out per gram?
(It takes 4.2 J of energy to raise the temperature of 1 g of water by 1°C.)

Energy = $100 \times 4.2 \times 5 = 2100\,\text{J}$

Energy/g = $2100/0.2 = \mathbf{10\,500\,J/g}$ (or 10.5 kJ/g)

The energy content of food is sometimes expressed in calories per 100 g.
1 calorie = 4.2 joules
Fats, oils and carbohydrates are 'high energy' foods and too much in your diet can cause obesity.

▶ **Measuring heats of reaction**

Many reactions take place in solution. We can find the energy involved by measuring the temperature change.
Then we can assume that it takes 4.2 joules of energy to raise the temperature of 1 g of solution by 1°C.
We can use this in displacement or in neutralisation reactions.

stir gently with a thermometer

poly(styrene) beaker

Example 2

25 cm³ of dilute hydrochloric acid was added to 25 cm³ of sodium hydroxide solution. The temperature rose by a maximum of 15°C. How much energy was released?

The temperature of 50 cm³ (which equals 50 g) of solution was raised by 15°C.

Energy = $50 \times 4.2 \times 15 = \mathbf{3150\,J}$

► Energy level diagrams

We can show energy changes in chemical reactions on an energy level diagram.

ΔH is the symbol for the energy change in a reaction.

ΔH **is negative** for an **exothermic** reaction.

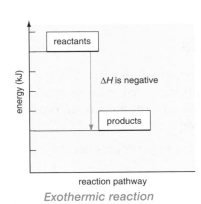

Exothermic reaction

ΔH **is positive** for an **endothermic** reaction.

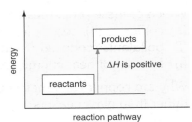

Endothermic reaction

Making new bonds gives out energy. It is an **exothermic** process.

Breaking bonds to start a reaction requires energy. It is an **endothermic** process.

- If the energy given out when new bonds form is *greater than* the energy needed to break the existing bonds, then the reaction is exothermic.
- If the energy given out when new bonds form is *less than* the energy needed to break the existing bonds, then the reaction is endothermic.
- To see the effect of a catalyst on activation energy, look back to page 67.

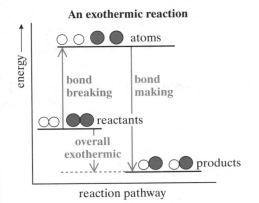

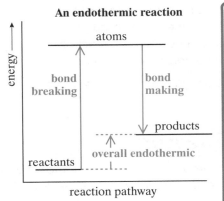

More in **Chemistry for You,** pages 192–202, 213.

► Calculating ΔH

- Bond energies are a measure of the *strength* of a bond.
- We can use bond energies to work out an approximate value of ΔH for a reaction.

Example 3

Calculate the approximate energy change accompanying the reaction between hydrogen and chlorine to make hydrogen chloride:

$$H_2 + Cl_2 \longrightarrow 2HCl$$

(Bond energy values are: H—H = 436 kJ/mol, Cl—Cl = 242 kJ/mol, H—Cl = 431 kJ/mol)

Bonds broken:

$+[1 \times (H—H)] + [1 \times (Cl—Cl)]$
$= +(436 + 242)$
$= +678$ kJ/mol

Bonds made:

$-(2 \times H—Cl)$
$= -(2 \times 431)$
$= -862$ kJ/mol

Add these two up to get the overall energy change:

$(+678) + (-862) \qquad = \mathbf{-184\ kJ/mol}$

Energy

Homework Questions

1 Which of these properties are important when considering a new fuel?
(a) colour   (b) cost   (c) availability   (d) ease of ignition   (e) ease of transportation
(f) pollutants produced on combustion   (g) the smoke produced   (h) the toxicity of the fuel
(i) amount of heat energy produced *(1 mark)*

2 Why are copper calorimeters used for experiments on the energy released when fuels burn rather than glass beakers? *(1 mark)*

3 (a) Calculate the total amount of energy transferred when 100 g of water has its temperature raised by 20 °C. (It takes 4.2 J of energy to raise the temperature of 1 g of water by 1°C.) *(3 marks)*
(b) The energy transferred in part (a) was produced by the combustion of 0.4 g ethanol. How much energy is released per gram of ethanol? *(3 marks)*
(c) Write the chemical equation for the combustion of ethanol (C_2H_5OH). *(4 marks)*

4 In an experiment, 20 cm³ of dilute nitric acid was neutralised by 18 cm³ of potassium hydroxide solution. If the temperature of the acid initially was 16°C and the highest temperature reached when the acid was neutralised was 24°C, calculate the energy released in the reaction. *(4 marks)*

5 (a) In this reaction: $Fe + CuSO_4 \longrightarrow FeSO_4 + Cu$, 0.5 g of iron filings reacted with 10 cm³ of dilute copper sulfate solution to produce copper. If the temperature rose by 6°C, calculate the amount of energy released. *(3 marks)*
(b) Is this an exothermic or endothermic reaction? *(1 mark)*
(c) Draw an energy level diagram for this reaction. *(1 mark)*

6 ΔH for a chemical reaction was calculated as +146 kJ/mol. Draw an energy level diagram to represent this reaction. *(1 mark)*

22 marks

Examination Question

At room temperature, hydrogen peroxide decomposes very slowly to form water and oxygen. The decomposition is speeded up when a catalyst is added.

[H] (a) The following equation represents the decomposition of hydrogen peroxide. The structural formulae of the chemicals involved are shown.

$$2\left(\begin{array}{c} O \\ H \quad O \end{array} \begin{array}{c} H \end{array} \right) \longrightarrow 2\left(\begin{array}{c} O \\ H \quad H \end{array} \right) + O = O$$

Use the following information about bond energies to answer this part of the question.

Bond	Bond energy (kJ)
O=O	498
O—O	146
H—O	464

(i) Calculate the energy needed to break all the bonds in the reactants.

....

....

.... kJ
(2 marks)

(ii) Calculate the energy released when new bonds are formed in the products.

....

....

.... kJ

(2 marks)

(iii) Calculate the energy change for this reaction.

....

.... kJ

(1 mark)

(iv) Is the reaction exothermic or endothermic? ....

Explain why.   ....

....

(1 mark)

(b) (i) What is meant by 'activation energy'?

....

....

(1 mark)

(ii) The energy level diagram for the decomposition of hydrogen peroxide into water and oxygen is shown below.

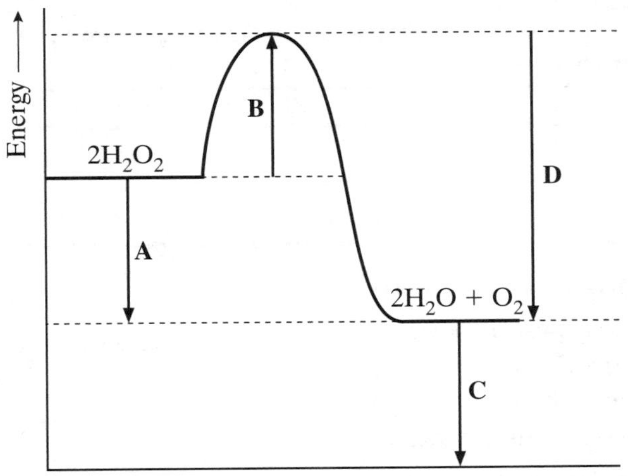

Which energy change, **A**, **B**, **C** or **D**, is the activation energy? .... *(1 mark)*

(iii) Explain, in terms of energy, how a catalyst makes hydrogen peroxide decompose more quickly.

....

....

....

(1 mark)

9 marks

Detection and identification

▶ **ThinkAbout:**

1. Do the atoms of metals form positively or negatively charged ions?
2. What is the formula of an aluminium ion (Al is in Group 3 in the Periodic Table)?
3. Name three halide ions.
4. What is the charge on a sulfate ion?
5. Give the formula of:
   a) ammonium sulfate   b) iron(III) nitrate.

▶ **Identifying negatively charged ions (anions)**

Here is a summary of the tests we can use to identify some common negatively charged ions (anions):

Anion	Test
Chloride (Cl^-)	Dissolve in dilute nitric acid, then a white precipitate forms with silver nitrate solution.
Bromide (Br^-)	Dissolve in dilute nitric acid, then a cream precipitate forms with silver nitrate solution.
Iodide (I^-)	Dissolve in dilute nitric acid, then a pale yellow precipitate forms with silver nitrate solution.
Sulfate (SO_4^{2-})	Dissolve in dilute hydrochloric acid, then a white precipitate of barium sulfate forms with barium chloride solution.
Nitrate (NO_3^-)	Add sodium hydroxide solution and aluminium powder. Then warm and test the gas given off (ammonia) with damp red litmus paper, which turns blue.
Carbonate (CO_3^{2-})	Add dilute acid, then pass the carbon dioxide gas through limewater, which turns milky (cloudy).

▶ **Two tell-tale carbonates**

- You can recognise **copper carbonate** because it turns from green to black (forming copper oxide) when heated.

$CuCO_3$ $\xrightarrow{\text{heat}}$ $CuO + CO_2$

- Heating **zinc carbonate** turns the white powder bright yellow. Then it goes white again when cool. It forms zinc oxide, when heated, which is responsible for the colour change.

$ZnCO_3$ $\xrightarrow{\text{heat}}$ hot $ZnO + CO_2$
$\xrightarrow{\text{cool}}$ ZnO

Answers:

▶ Identifying positively charged ions (cations)

Here are the positive ions (cations) we can test with **sodium hydroxide solution**:

Precipitate of copper hydroxide
$Cu^{2+}(aq) + 2OH^-(aq) \rightarrow Cu(OH)_2(s)$

Precipitate of iron(II) hydroxide
$Fe^{2+}(aq) + 2OH^-(aq) \rightarrow Fe(OH)_2(s)$

Cation	Result of adding sodium hydroxide solution
Copper(II)	Pale blue precipitate
Iron(II)	Dirty green precipitate (which turns rusty brown if left)
Iron(III)	Rusty brown precipitate
Aluminium	White precipitate which dissolves in excess sodium hydroxide
Magnesium	White precipitate
Calcium	White precipitate

Precipitate of iron(III) hydroxide
$Fe^{3+}(aq) + 3OH^-(aq) \rightarrow Fe(OH)_3(s)$

▶ Ammonium ions

(NH_4^+) give off ammonia gas when we heat them with sodium hydroxide solution. Ammonia is the only common alkaline gas. We test for ammonia with damp red litmus paper: it turns blue.

Testing ammonia gas

▶ Flame tests

Some metal ions also give out coloured light when we heat them in a Bunsen flame:

Cation	Colour of flame test
Sodium	Bright yellow
Lithium	Red (scarlet)
Calcium	Brick red
Potassium	Lilac
Barium	Apple green

lithium
(scarlet red)

barium
(apple green)

sodium
(bright yellow)

calcium
(brick red)

potassium
(lilac)

N.B. Magnesium ions do not produce a coloured flame.

More in *Chemistry for You,* pages 360–363, 368–369.

Detection and identification

Homework Questions

1 An unknown substance gave a bright yellow flame test. When dilute hydrochloric was added to the solid, carbon dioxide gas was evolved. What is the name of this substance? *(1 mark)*

2 Name the only common alkaline gas. *(1 mark)*

3 Which carbonate turns yellow on heating, only to go white again as it cools? *(1 mark)*

4 An unknown solid was dissolved in water. Two tests were then carried out:
1. Sodium hydroxide solution was added to a solution of the solid. It formed a rusty brown solid.
2. Sodium hydroxide solution was added to a solution of the solid followed by aluminium powder. On heating ammonia was evolved.

Identify the unknown solid. *(1 mark)*

5 Copy and complete this equation:
$$CuCO_3 \longrightarrow \text{...........} + \text{...........}$$ *(2 marks)*

6 What would you see if dilute nitric acid, followed by silver nitrate solution was added to a colourless solution of sodium bromide? *(1 mark)*

7 Which ion gives a lilac flame test? *(1 mark)*

8 Copy and complete this equation:
$$CuSO_4 \, (aq) + BaCl_2 \, (aq) \longrightarrow \text{...........} + \text{...........}$$ *(2 marks)*

9 Sodium chloride and sodium iodide are both white, crystalline solids with high melting points. Describe a chemical test which could identify these compounds. *(1 mark)*

10 Barium sulfate is a white insoluble, poisonous solid. Lead sulfate is also a white insoluble, poisonous solid. What test could you do, to identify which solid was barium sulfate? *(1 mark)*

11 How could you distinguish between the white solids magnesium chloride and aluminium chloride? *(1 mark)*

13 marks

Examination Questions

1 The flow diagram shows some reactions of iron.

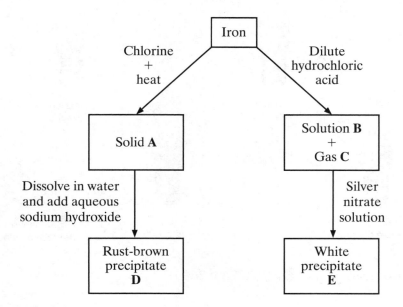

Choose from the list below to answer parts (a) to (e).

hydrogen   **iron(II) chloride**   **iron(III) chloride**
iron(II) hydroxide   **iron(III) hydroxide**   **oxygen**
silver chloride   **silver nitrate**

(a) Solid **A** is ....

(b) Solution **B** is ....

(c) Gas **C** is ....

(d) Rust-brown precipitate **D** is ....

(e) White precipitate **E** is ....

(5 marks)

5 marks

2   Chemical tests are used to identify compounds.

(a) What colour is produced by sodium compounds in flame tests?

.... (1 mark)

(b) Chemical tests are carried out on these substances.

ammonium chloride	**copper bromide**	**magnesium sulfate**
potassium nitrate	**sodium nitrate**	**zinc carbonate**

Complete each sentence by choosing the correct substance from the box.
You may use each substance **once**, **more than once** or **not at all**.
The substance which

(i)   reacts with dilute hydrochloric acid to produce carbon dioxide gas is

.... (1 mark)

(ii) in solution reacts with sodium hydroxide solution to form a blue precipitate is

.... (1 mark)

(iii) in solution reacts with barium chloride solution, in the presence of dilute hydrochloric acid, to form a white precipitate is

.... (1 mark)

(iv) dissolves in dilute nitric acid, then reacts with silver nitrate to form a cream coloured precipitate is

.... (1 mark)

(v) turns yellow when heated, but changes back to white when allowed to cool down is

.... (1 mark)

(c) State what you **see** when sodium chloride solution reacts with silver nitrate solution in the presence of dilute nitric acid.

.... (1 mark)

7 marks

Analysis

> ### ThinkAbout:
> 1. What elements are found in a hydrocarbon?
> 2. What are the products formed when a hydrocarbon is burned completely in plenty of oxygen?
> 3. What do we call the reaction in question 2?
> 4. What is the relative formula mass of:
>   a) CO_2 and b) H_2O?
>   (C = 12, H = 1, O = 16)

> ### Chemical analysis of an organic compound
> We can also analyse an unknown organic compound chemically to find out its formula.
> We burn the compound in oxygen. Then the gases made are passed through absorption tubes, which absorb water vapour formed and carbon dioxide. The gases are analysed by machines before and after they enter the absorption tubes. They tell us the mass of water and carbon dioxide produced.

> ### Organic compounds
> When we heat an organic compound, it burns or chars.
>
> Some organic compounds are unsaturated. Their molecules contains C=C bonds. We can detect these using bromine water. If the solution is decolourised, the compound is unsaturated.

H

Example

A sample of a compound was found to contain carbon, hydrogen and oxygen.
Its relative formula mass was found to be 92.
On complete combustion of 9.2 g of the compound in oxygen, 17.6 g of carbon dioxide and 10.8 g of water vapour were absorbed in tubes.
What is the chemical formula of the compound?
(A_r values: C = 12, H = 1, O = 16)

First we have to find the mass of carbon and hydrogen from the data provided about CO_2 and H_2O.

So how much carbon is there in 17.6 g of carbon dioxide?
The relative formula mass of CO_2 is 12 + (16 × 2) = 44 (of which 12 is made up of carbon).
So we have $(\frac{12}{44})$ × 17.6 g of carbon in the unknown compound = **4.8 g of carbon**.

And how much hydrogen is in 10.8 g of H_2O?
The relative formula mass of H_2O is (2 × 1) + 16 = 18 (of which 2 is made up of hydrogen).
So we have $(\frac{2}{18})$ × 10.8 g of hydrogen in the unknown compound = **1.2 g of hydrogen**.

The rest of the compound, i.e. 9.2 − (4.8 + 1.2), must be oxygen.
So we have 3.2 g of oxygen.

Now we do the calculation to find the *simplest ratio of moles* which will give us the **empirical formula**:

C	:	H	:	O
4.8 ÷ 12	:	1.2 ÷ 1	:	3.2 ÷ 16
0.4	:	1.2	:	0.2 (divide everything by 0.2 to get simplest ratio)
2	:	6	:	1

So the empirical formula is **C_2H_6O**

This is not the actual molecular formula because we are told its relative formula mass is 92.
The relative formula mass of C_2H_6O would be (2 × 12) + (6 × 1) + (1 × 16) = 46
92 = 46 × 2, so the actual formula of the unknown compound is (C_2H_6O × 2) = **$C_4H_{12}O_2$**

▶ Instrumental analysis

Nowadays we can use modern instruments to detect and measure tiny amounts of elements and compounds in very small samples. The instruments are sensitive and give accurate results quickly. These machines are used to monitor and control water quality, but have also found many other uses, for example in forensic science and in hospitals.

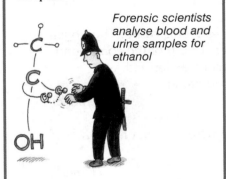

Forensic scientists analyse blood and urine samples for ethanol

▶ Atomic absorption spectrometers

H

Spectrometers are expensive machines that analyse the energy (in the form of electromagnetic radiation, such as light) absorbed or given out by a sample. Atomic spectrometers are used to detect which elements are in a sample. The sample is heated in a flame. Any molecules are broken down at this stage. The energy from the flame causes electrons in the atoms of the sample to jump into higher energy levels (shells).

Each element has its own characteristic set of energies that it absorbs. We can see these as dark lines in a spectrum or as troughs when analysed by a detector and fed into a computer.

This method can be used to tell us which elements are present by matching the spectrum to a database of known elements stored on the computer. It can also show how much of each element is present. For example, we can now detect toxic mercury in a sample of water down to traces as low as 0.000 000 001 g!

Atomic absorption spectrometers are used in other industries, besides the water industry, to monitor samples. For example, the steel industry can carefully analyse the amounts of trace elements present in steel to control its quality.

▶ Visible–ultra-violet spectroscopy

These instruments are used to analyse which compounds are present in a sample. The sample is not broken up by any harsh treatment in the machine, such as heating it in a flame. Light is shone on the sample, then the result is analysed to see which wavelengths are absorbed.

The spectrum can be matched or 'fingerprinted' against known samples and then the sample identified.

H

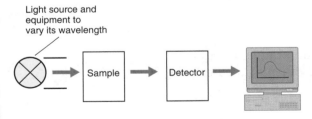

Light source and equipment to vary its wavelength

If a compound does not absorb light in the visible–ultra-violet part of the spectrum, this technique will not work. However, the compound can be reacted with other compounds to give products that do absorb light in the right range. Then these compounds can be detected. This method is used in the water industry to analyse levels of nitrate and phosphate pollutants in water supplies.

More in *Chemistry for You*, pages 365–367.

▶ Other instrumental methods

H

The following are useful methods for identifying compounds:
- infra-red spectrometry
- nuclear magnetic resonance
- gas–liquid chromatography (this can also separate mixtures before analysis in another instrument)
- mass spectrometry (also useful for identifying elements).

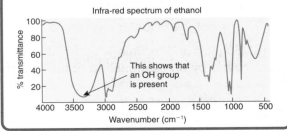

Infra-red spectrum of ethanol

This shows that an OH group is present

Analysis

Homework Questions

1 Which compounds are formed when any hydrocarbon burns in a plentiful supply of oxygen? *(2 marks)*

2 Copy and complete these equations:
(a) $CH_4 + 2O_2 \longrightarrow$ .... + ... *(2 marks)*
(b) .... + ... $\longrightarrow 3CO_2 + 4H_2O$ *(2 marks)*
(c) $C_5H_{12} +$ .... $\longrightarrow 5CO_2 +$ .... *(2 marks)*

3 (a) How much carbon is there in 7.20 g of carbon dioxide? (A_r values: C=12, O=16) *(1 mark)*
(b) How much hydrogen is there in 7.56 g of water? (A_r values: H = 1) *(1 mark)*

[H] **4** A sample of an organic compound was found to contain only the elements carbon, hydrogen and oxygen. Its relative formula mass was determined as 88. When 17.6 g of the compound was burned in oxygen, 35.2 g of carbon dioxide and 14.4 g of water was formed.
Find (a) the empirical formula, and (b) the molecular formula of the organic compound. *(2 marks)*

5 Look up in your textbook, or research the Internet, and write a paragraph about how each of these techniques are used:
(a) Visible / ultra-violet spectroscopy. *(1 mark)*
(b) Infra-red spectrometry. *(1 mark)*
(c) Nuclear magnetic resonance spectroscopy. *(1 mark)*
(d) Gas–liquid chromatography. *(1 mark)*
(e) Mass spectrometry. *(1 mark)* $\overline{18}$
(f) Atomic absorption spectroscopy. *(1 mark)* marks

Examination Questions

1 Two substances (**A** and **B**) have the same molecular formula, C_2H_6O.
One substance is an alcohol (CH_3CH_2OH) and the other is an ether (CH_3OCH_3).
Their structural formulae are shown below:

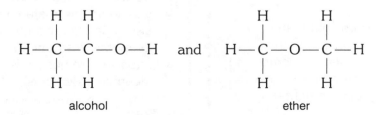

alcohol   ether

(a) Suggest and explain why the alcohol and the ether cannot be distinguished from each other by an examination of their combustion products.

....

.... *(2 marks)*

H (b) **All the information needed to answer part (b) is given in the question.**
Read the information in the box about infra-red spectroscopy.

> Infra-red spectroscopy is an instrumental method of analysis, which is used **to identify bonds and functional groups** in organic compounds.
>
> When infra-red light is shone through an organic compound, some of the light is absorbed. When this happens, less of the light is transmitted and this produces a pattern of troughs called an infra-red spectrum. Different bonds and functional groups absorb different amounts of infra-red light and produce different patterns.
>
> Identification of a particular bond or functional group is made by matching it to its absorption range in the infra-red spectrum.

The table shows the approximate absorption range of some bonds.

Bond	Approximate absorption range
C—H	2850–3000
C—C	800–1000
C—O	1000–1300
O—H	3230–3550

The infra-red spectra of substances **A** and **B** are shown below.

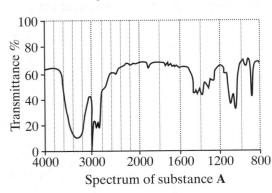

Spectrum of substance **A**

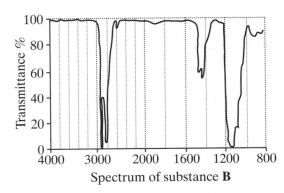

Spectrum of substance **B**

Use the information given to suggest why spectrum **A** is that of the alcohol and spectrum **B** is that of the ether.

Explanation: ....

....

....

(2 marks)

4 marks

2 (a) Name an instrumental method of analysis that might be used to detect a drug in the urine of an athlete.

.... *(1 mark)*

(b) Describe how advances in technology have assisted in the development of instrumental methods for the detection and identification of elements and compounds.

....

....

....

....

(2 marks)

3 marks

Answers on page 116

Getting the Grades – Energy changes

Try this question, then compare your answer with the two examples opposite ▶

This question is about the energy transfers that take place when a chemical reaction happens.

(a) A student was asked to investigate the amount of energy transferred when hydrochloric acid reacts with alkalis. The student thought the same amount of energy would be transferred when hydrochloric acid reacts with potassium hydroxide or sodium hydroxide. To find out the student measured the temperature change when hydrochloric acid was reacted with each alkali in turn. The apparatus used and the results for sodium hydroxide are shown in the diagram.

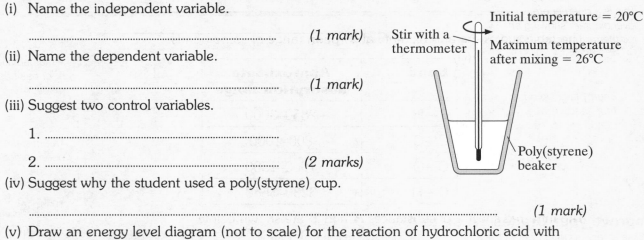

(i) Name the independent variable.

.... *(1 mark)*

(ii) Name the dependent variable.

.... *(1 mark)*

(iii) Suggest two control variables.

1. ....

2. .... *(2 marks)*

(iv) Suggest why the student used a poly(styrene) cup.

.... *(1 mark)*

(v) Draw an energy level diagram (not to scale) for the reaction of hydrochloric acid with sodium hydroxide.

hydrochloric acid + sodium hydroxide ⟶ sodium chloride + water

(3 marks)

(vi) What temperature change would you expect for the reaction of hydrochloric acid with potassium hydroxide?

.... *(1 mark)*

H (b) Hydrochloric acid is formed by dissolving hydrogen chloride gas in water. Hydrogen chloride can be made by reacting hydrogen gas directly with chlorine gas. The equation for this reaction is:

$$H_2 \text{ (g)} + Cl_2 \text{ (g)} \longrightarrow 2HCl \text{ (g)}$$

The relevant bond energies are given below:

H—H is 436 kJ/mol; Cl—Cl is 242 kJ/mol; H—Cl is 431 kJ/mol.

(i) Use the bond energy values to calculate the energy transferred in this reaction.

....

....

.... *(3 marks)*

(ii) Explain, in terms of bond energies, why this is an exothermic reaction.

....

.... *(2 marks)*

14 marks

GRADE 'A' ANSWER

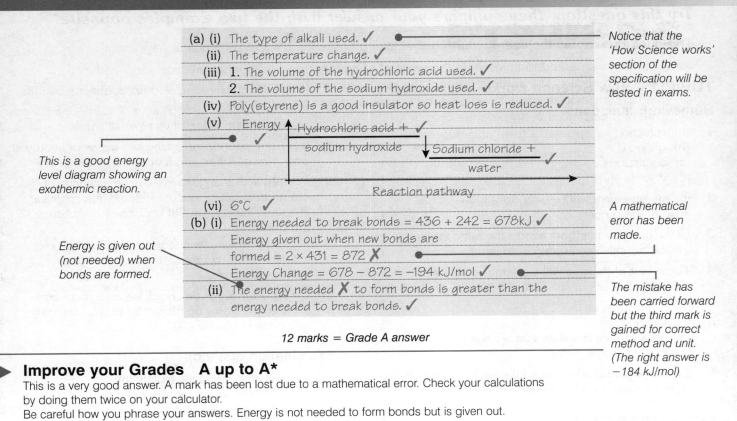

(a) (i) The type of alkali used. ✓

    (ii) The temperature change. ✓

    (iii) 1. The volume of the hydrochloric acid used. ✓

         2. The volume of the sodium hydroxide used. ✓

    (iv) Poly(styrene) is a good insulator so heat loss is reduced. ✓

    (v) ✓

Energy ↑

Hydrochloric acid + sodium hydroxide ✓

↓ Sodium chloride + water ✓

Reaction pathway

    (vi) 6°C ✓

(b) (i) Energy needed to break bonds = 436 + 242 = 678kJ ✓

      Energy given out when new bonds are formed = 2 × 431 = 872 ✗

      Energy Change = 678 − 872 = −194 kJ/mol ✓

    (ii) The energy needed ✗ to form bonds is greater than the energy needed to break bonds. ✓

Notice that the 'How Science works' section of the specification will be tested in exams.

This is a good energy level diagram showing an exothermic reaction.

Energy is given out (not needed) when bonds are formed.

A mathematical error has been made.

The mistake has been carried forward but the third mark is gained for correct method and unit. (The right answer is −184 kJ/mol)

12 marks = Grade A answer

▶ Improve your Grades   A up to A*

This is a very good answer. A mark has been lost due to a mathematical error. Check your calculations by doing them twice on your calculator.

Be careful how you phrase your answers. Energy is not needed to form bonds but is given out.

GRADE 'C' ANSWER

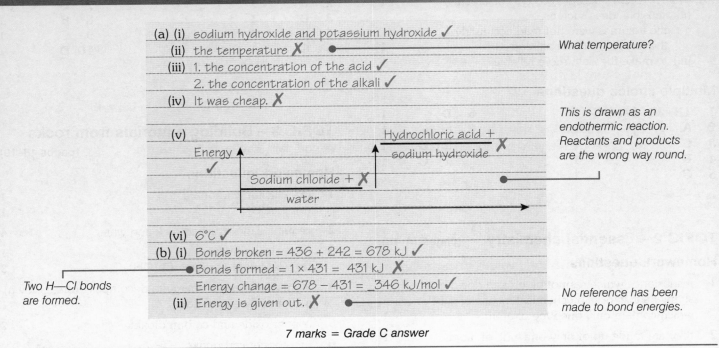

(a) (i) sodium hydroxide and potassium hydroxide ✓

    (ii) the temperature ✗

    (iii) 1. the concentration of the acid ✓

         2. the concentration of the alkali ✓

    (iv) It was cheap. ✗

    (v)

Energy ↑ ✓

Hydrochloric acid + sodium hydroxide ✗

Sodium chloride + ✗ water

    (vi) 6°C ✓

(b) (i) Bonds broken = 436 + 242 = 678 kJ ✓

      Bonds formed = 1 × 431 = 431 kJ ✗

      Energy change = 678 − 431 = 346 kJ/mol ✓

    (ii) Energy is given out. ✗

What temperature?

This is drawn as an endothermic reaction. Reactants and products are the wrong way round.

Two H—Cl bonds are formed.

No reference has been made to bond energies.

7 marks = Grade C answer

▶ Improve your Grades   C up to B

An exothermic reaction gives out energy to the surroundings so the temperature on the thermometer goes up. The reactants have lost this energy when they form products. Thus the energy level of the products is lower than the reactants.

Note that part (b) of this question would only appear in a Higher Tier examination.

Examination answers

TOPIC 1 – How Science works   (pages 10–11)
Homework questions
1 (a) categoric   1
   (b) ordered   1
   (c) continuous   1
   (d) discrete   1

2 the measurement will be very close to the actual mass of the copper   1

3 all the measurements are almost the same and a suitably sensitive measuring instrument was used   1

4 The colour of the cola will mask the colour of the indicator. The colour seen will not give the pH of the cola.   1

5 (a) temperature   1
   (b) mass of copper sulfate that dissolves   1
   (c) e.g. volume of water   1

6 if all the laboratories obtained the same result then the methods used must be reliable   1

Examination question
(a) the oxygen in the measuring cylinder reacted with the iron to form iron oxide   1
water rose to take the place of the oxygen in the measuring cylinder   1
(b) (i) $19.75 \ cm^3$ (accept $19.8 \ cm^3$ or $20 \ cm^3$)   1
   (ii) sensible ideas such as:
     the volumes were not read accurately
     the oxygen had not all reacted   1
   (iii) to make the data more reliable   1

Multiple choice questions
1 **1B, 2D, 3A, 4C**   4   6 **D**   1
2 **A**   1   7 (a) **C**   1
3 **C**   1   (b) **D**   1
4 **B**   1   (c) **C**   1
5 **C**   1

TOPIC 2 – Essential chemistry   (pages 14–15)
Homework questions
1 a substance which cannot be broken down into simpler substances by chemical means or substances which contain only one type of atom   1

2 they are made up of only one type of atom   1

3 Al, S, Br, He, Ni   5

4 hydrogen, magnesium, carbon, chlorine, calcium   5

5 some elements have symbols derived from their Latin names   1

6 beryllium, magnesium, calcium, strontium, barium   5

7 Elements contain just one kind of atom. Compounds always contain at least two types of atoms.   2

8 it is a compound, containing two atoms of hydrogen, one atom of sulfur, and four atoms of oxygen   1

9 In a physical change there may be a change of state, but no new substances are formed. In a chemical change there is always at least one new substance formed.   1
e.g. physical – melting, boiling, evaporation, etc.   1
e.g. chemical – combustion, neutralisation, displacement, etc.   1

10 the equation is not balanced, because there are two oxygen atoms on the left-hand side, but only one on the right-hand side   1

Examination question
(a) *Elements* – copper, aluminium   2
   Compounds – pure water and salt   2
   Mixtures – milk and sand   2
(b) salt   1

Multiple choice questions
1 **B**   1   6 **A**   1
2 **B**   1   7 **C**   1
3 **D**   1   8 **B**   1
4 **C**   1   9 **C**   1
5 **C**   1   10 **D**   1

TOPIC 3 – Building materials from rocks
                                            (pages 18–19)
Homework questions
1 (a) calcium carbonate   1
   (b) $CaCO_3$ 1

2 cement, sand, crushed rock and water   4

3 (a) calcium hydroxide   1
   (b) $CaO + H_2O \longrightarrow Ca(OH)_2$ 3

4 the use of thermal energy to decompose (break down) a chemical compound   1

5 copper oxide and carbon dioxide   2

6 (a) copper carbonate $\longrightarrow$
        copper oxide + carbon dioxide   1
   (b) $CuCO_3 \longrightarrow CuO + CO_2$ 1

7 sand   1

8 to neutralise the acidity caused by acid rain   1

Examination answers

9 water and sand   2

10 The solution would turn milky (or cloudy). This is because the carbon dioxide is reacting with the calcium hydroxide solution to produce a precipitate of calcium carbonate. The white calcium carbonate is insoluble, so causing the 'milkiness' in the liquid.   2

Examination question

(a) calcium, carbon, oxygen   3
(b) there are chemical bonds   1
     joining the different elements   1
(c) (i)   calcium carbonate   1
     (ii)   calcium oxide / carbon dioxide   1
     (iii) thermal decomposition   1
     (iv) carbon dioxide   1

Multiple choice questions

1   C   1   **6**   B   1
2   A   1   **7**   D   1
3   A   1   **8**   C   1
4   B   1   **9**   D   1
5   D   1   **10**   D   1

TOPIC 4 – Useful products from metal ores
(pages 22–23)

Homework questions

1 sodium, aluminium, zinc, tin, lead, copper   6

2 It forms very strong bonds with the elements it bonds with. These are very hard to break, so need a lot of energy.   1

3 the carbon reduces the lead oxide to lead, removing its oxygen   1

4 iron ore, coke, limestone, air   4

5 to make the steel stainless   1

6 (a) *any six from:* e.g. copper, nickel, iron, zinc, cobalt, magnesium, vanadium, chromium, titanium, etc.   6
    (b) high melting point, good thermal conductor, good electrical conductor, malleable, ductile, strong   6

7 the passage of an electric current through a liquid, accompanied by a reaction at the electrodes   1

8 (a) a mixture of two or more metals   1
    (b) *any two from:* e.g. duralumin, alnico, brass, bronze, etc.   2
    (c) e.g. in making spectacle frames   1

9 strong, not corrosive, easily shaped, durable   1

10 low density, malleable, not corrosive, durable   1

11 malleable, strong, does not easily corrode, durable   1

12 carbon behaves like a metal in that it can reduce the oxides of metals less reactive than itself   1

Examination question

(a) mixture
     of two or more metals   2
(b) steel   1
(c) stronger / harder   1
(d) copper and zinc   1

Multiple choice questions

1   D   1   **6**   D   1
2   A   1   **7**   A   1
3   C   1   **8**   B   1
4   B   1   **9**   D   1
5   C   1   **10**   B   1

TOPIC 5 – Useful products from oil
(pages 26–27)

Homework questions

1 salt solution contains only one solvent (water), whereas crude oil is a mixture of many different substances   1

2 a compound containing only hydrogen and carbon   1

3 they all have different boiling points   1

4 petrol, kerosene, diesel, fuel oil, bitumen   5

5 the alkanes only have single bonds   1

6 C_8H_{18} 1

7 C_5H_{12} 1

8 (a) water and carbon dioxide   2
    (b) carbon monoxide   1
    (c) it combines with haemoglobin in blood to stop the uptake of oxygen   1

9 carbon dioxide   1

10 sulfur dioxide (formed as a result of sulfur impurities in fossil fuels which are oxidised during combustion)   1

11 *For example:* Greenhouse gases allow **sunlight** to enter the **atmosphere.** When sunlight strikes the Earth's surface and warms it up. As the Earth cools down it **re-radiates** some energy back into space as infra-red **radiation.** This radiation can be **absorbed** by greenhouse gases and heats up the atmosphere.   5

Examination question

(a) hydrogen, carbon   2
(b) (i)   water   1
     (ii) limewater   1

Multiple choice questions

1   D   1   **6**   A   1
2   A   1   **7**   C   1
3   D   1   **8**   C   1
4   D   1   **9**   D   1
5   C   1   **10**   D   1

Examination answers

TOPIC 6 – Polymers and ethanol from oil
(pages 32–33)

Homework questions

1   petrol   1
2   to meet the demand for lighter fractions e.g. petrol   1
3   ethane has a single bond between its two carbon atoms, whereas ethene has a double bond between its carbon atoms   1
4   C_4H_8 1
5   the double bond makes it much more reactive   1
6   ethanol   1
7   poly(ethene)   1
8   (a) chloroethene   1
    (b) polychloroethene (PVC)   1
9   poly(propene)   1
10 e.g. milk crates   1
11 intelligent packaging includes time and temperature indicators, embedding microchips or nanosensors in polymers, and radio frequency identification technology   2

Examination question

(a) ethanol **1**
(b) $C_2H_4 + H_2O \longrightarrow C_2H_5OH$
    (C_2H_6O) 1
(c) because it is made from ethene which is made from **crude oil**   1

Multiple choice questions

1   1B, 2A, 3C, 4D   4   5   A   1
2   B   1   6   D   1
3   C   1   7   C   1
4   B   1

TOPIC 7 – Plant oils   **(pages 36–37)**

Homework questions

1   Because oil and water do not mix. They are immiscible liquids.   1
2   immiscible means two liquids, which do not mix together   1
3   A solution contains dissolved particles of solute, which are too small to see even with a powerful microscope. An emulsion contains suspended particles of oil in a liquid (or liquid in an oil). These particles can often be seen under small magnification.   1
4   hydrophilic – 'tending to dissolve in, mix with, or be wetted by water' – a water-loving molecule   1
    hydrophobic – a water-hating molecule   1

5   emulsifier: lecithin in egg yolk   1
6   food colourings: e.g. E102 Tartrazine, E110 Sunset yellow, E120 Carmine, E123 Amaranth   2
7   'Sudan' group dyes have been found to be carcinogenic   1
8   a poly-unsaturate is a long hydrocarbon molecule / chain containing many double bonds   1
9   Oils are liquid at room temperature, fats are solid at room temperature. Oils are less viscous than fats and have weaker forces between their molecules, because they do not pack together so easily.   2
10 (a) a substance of biological origin which can be used as a fuel   1
    (b) *one from:* because fossil fuels are running out; the plants from which it is made absorb carbon dioxide; it does not contribute to acid rain, it is degradable   1

Examination question

(a) (i) **B**   (ii) **D**   (iii) **A**   (iv) **C**   4
(b) add bromine water to the compound in a test-tube and shake the tube
    if the orange/yellow bromine water decolourises, the compound is unsaturated   1

Multiple choice questions

1   B   1   6   D   1
2   B   1   7   A   1
3   C   1   8   B   1
4   D   1   9   C   1
5   C   1   10   A   1

TOPIC 8 – Earth and its atmosphere
(pages 40–41)

Homework questions

1   Los Angeles is on a plate boundary so gets frequent earthquakes. UK is not on a plate boundary, so does not often get earthquakes.   1
2   crust and upper part of mantle   1
3   scientists later found evidence of movement of tectonic plates beneath the oceans   1
4   volcanoes   1
5   plants appeared and began to photosynthesise, producing oxygen   1
6   water vapour produced by volcanic action cooled and condensed to form the oceans   1
7   (a) Burning fossil fuels adds carbon dioxide to the air, but it is removed by dissolving in oceans and by photosynthesis, so the proportion is approximately in balance.   1

Examination answers

(b) 1850 (approx.) was the start of the industrial revolution   **1**

(c) Carbon dioxide is thought to be most likely cause of global warming. As the Earth's average temperature increases, ice caps will eventually melt, causing worldwide flooding.   **1**

8 they are chemically unreactive   **1**

9 (a) the Noble gases (Group 0)   **1**
  (b) krypton, xenon and radon   **3**

Examination question

any two from: the amount of carbon dioxide is much lower; the amount of oxygen is much higher; the amount of nitrogen is much higher; there is a lower proportion of 'other gases'   **2**

Multiple choice questions

1	C	1	**6**	D	1
2	C	1	**7**	A	1
3	B	1	**8**	C	1
4	A	1	**9**	A	1
5	D	1	**10**	B	1

TOPIC 9 – Atomic structure   (pages 46–47)
Homework questions

1 electron: JJ Thomson 1897; proton: E Rutherford 1911; neutron: J Chadwick 1932   **3**

2 (a) protons and neutrons   **2**
  (b) electron   **1**

3 (a) potassium – 2,8,8,1
  (b) carbon – 2,6
  (c) sulfur – 2,8,6
  (d) argon – 2,8,8   **4**

4

Particle name	Mass of particle	Charge
electron	**almost 0**	**−1**
proton	1	+1
neutron	**1**	**0**

  5

5 the numbers would be far too small to be convenient to use   **1**

6 *atomic number:* number of protons (= number of electrons); *mass number:* number of protons + number of neutrons   **2**

7 element; protons; electrons; neutrons   **4**

Examination questions

1 A = nucleus, B = electron, C = neutron   **3**

2 (a) (i) neutron (ii) nucleus (iii) electron   **3**
  (b) (i) 100 (ii) 157   **2**

3 (a) A has no neutrons, B has 1 neutron   **2**
  (b) isotopes   **1**

4 correct structure showing 2, 7 gets 1 mark   **1**

TOPIC 10 – Bonding   (pages 50–51)
Homework questions

1 an ion is an electronically charged particle made when atoms transfer 1, 2, or 3 electrons   **1**

2 (a) Na^+, Cl^-
  (b) Mg^{2+}, O^{2-}
  (c) K^+, Br^-
  (d) Ca^{2+}, Cl^-
  (e) Al^{3+}, Cl^- **5**

3 ionic involves metals and non-metals, covalent involves only non-metals; ionic involves transfer of electrons, covalent involves only sharing of electrons   **2**

4 Electron diagram showing correct number of energy levels / shells with correct number of electrons. One pair of electrons in shared energy level / shell between hydrogen and chlorine.   **1**

5 Electron diagram showing correct number of energy levels / shells with correct number of electrons. Two pairs of electrons in shared energy levels / shells between carbon and oxygen atoms.   **1**

6 the delocalised electrons move along the wire towards the positive terminal   **1**

7 In ionic bonding metals and non-metals are involved in bonding. In metallic bonding only metals are involved.
In ionic bonding electrons are transferred. In metallic bonding electrons move but are not lost to the positive metal ions.   **2**

Examination questions

1 (a) all electron shells filled with 18 electrons, arranged 2,8,8   **1**
  (b) loses two electrons from its highest energy level / outer shell / loses both outer electrons   **1**

2 Ca loses two electrons   **1**
each F atom gains 1 electron   **1**
forming full outer shell / stable electronic arrangement   **1**
giving the ions Ca^{2+} and F^- **1**
strong attraction between opposite charges   **1**

3 (a) covalent   **1**
  (b) made of molecules / when non-metals react / both atoms can gain electrons by sharing   **2**

TOPIC 11 – Structures   (pages 54–55)
Homework questions

1 sodium chloride exists as a giant ionic structure with millions of ions, not as a simple molecule   **1**

2 In a giant ionic lattice the ions cannot move (other than to vibrate) so cannot carry an electric current. When molten, the ions are set free, and so they can then carry charge. 1

3 Simple covalent molecules are not made of ions. Ions are needed to carry charge. 1

4 (a) potassium nitrate 1
(b) it is ionic, the rest are not 1

5 diamond can be thought of as a giant covalent molecule 1

6 They have different structures. Diamond has no free electrons. Graphite has some delocalised electrons, hence graphite is a conductor, diamond is not. 1

7 (a) This is science on a very small scale. These molecules measure in the region of 10^{-9} m, or one nanometre – hence the term 'nano-science'. 1
(b) A nanobot is a microscopic robot on the nanoscale. 1
(c) Nanobots could be used to carry out surgery on humans, on the microscopic scale. 1
(d) Nanocluster – e.g. a bucky ball, can be used to give metals superconductivity.
Nanotube – A group of carbon atoms shaped into a tube, which may be used in making new materials in the future e.g. superfast computer parts, drug delivery systems, etc. 2

8 Metals are giant lattice structures made of metal ions, which are surrounded by a sea of mobile electrons (called delocalised electrons). Hence most of them have high melting points and all of them conduct electricity. 2

Examination questions

1 molecules / molecular compound 1
strong forces or bonds within molecules 1
weak forces between molecules 1

2 (a) (i) strong electrostatic forces of attraction 1
which operate in all directions 1
(ii) increased vibration / sufficient energy to break the bonds in the rigid structure 1
ions become free to move about 1
(iii) the ions are free to carry charge through the liquid 1
(b) stronger attractive forces between atoms 1
each carbon atom forms strong covalent bonds with four neighbouring atoms 1

3 (a) made of layers of carbon atoms 1
has weak forces between layers 1
so that the layers can slide over each other 1
(b) each carbon atom forms 3 covalent bonds 1
leaving one electron from each atom that is delocalised 1
these delocalised electrons conduct electricity along the layers of carbon atoms 1

TOPIC 12 – Chemical calculations (pages 58–59)

Homework questions

1 a mole is the relative formula mass of a substance in grams 1

2 (a) 40 g   (b) 56 g   (c) 111 g 3

3 (a) 1 atom of calcium, 1 atom of carbon, 3 atoms of oxygen, so RFM = $40 + 12 + (16 \times 3) = 100$ 1
(b) $(23 \times 2) + 12 + (16 \times 3) = 106$ 1
(c) 0.1 mole 1
(d) 53 g 1

4 (a) $\%N = \frac{14}{17} \times 100 = 82.3\%$
(b) $\%N = \frac{28}{80} = 35\%$ 2

5 446 tonnes PbO gives 414 tonnes Pb 1

6 1.6 g oxygen 1

7 NaCl 1

Examination questions

1 (a) 56 g
(b) 44 tonnes 2

2 (a) carbon monoxide 1
(b) reduction 1
(c) 160 2
[112 + 48 = 1 mark]

3 (a) sodium is very reactive so would react with oxygen in air 1
(b) sodium is more reactive than titanium 1
(c) 144 3
[$TiCl_4 = 190 = 1$ mark. Another correct step in calculation e.g. 570/190 = 1 mark]

4 $N_2H_4 = 32$ g 1
would make (2×17) g = 34 g of NH_3 1

5

C	:	H	:	O
$\frac{60}{12}$	:	$\frac{4.48}{1}$	:	$\frac{35.52}{16}$
5	:	4.48	:	2.22
9	:	8	:	4

3

TOPIC 13 – Reversible reactions (pages 62–63)

Homework questions

1 one in which the reaction can proceed in both directions 1

2 (a) water + anhydrous copper sulfate
$\longrightarrow$ copper sulfate 1
(b) $5H_2O + CuSO_4 \longrightarrow CuSO_4.5H_2O$ 1

3 (a) the white powder 'disappears' (turns to a colourless gas / mixture of gases) 1
(b) the white solid reforms 1

4 (a) no 1
(b) at dynamic equilibrium, reactants are continually turning into products at the same rate as products are turning into reactants 1

Examination answers

5 (a) Germany – late 19th and early 20th century   1
    (b) the government wanted to make ammonia from raw materials readily available to them (instead of relying on imports that could be cut off in the event of war)   1
    (c) because it makes millions of tonnes of fertiliser every year to feed the world   1

6 Most plants cannot absorb nitrogen directly. It is too unreactive.   1

7 to speed up the rate of the reaction   1

8 (a) NH_4NO_3 1
    (b) $NH_3 + HNO_3 \longrightarrow NH_4NO_3$ 1

Examination questions

1 (a) Reaction **1** takes place at **high** temperature
       Reaction **2** takes place at **low** temperature   1
    (b) reversible   1
    (c) to prevent ammonia and hydrogen chloride gases escaping   1

2 (a) (i)   **A** = air; **B** = natural gas / methane   2
       (ii) catalyst / speeds up reaction   1
    (b) $3H_2$ / $2NH_3$ 1
    (c) **C** = nitric acid   1
    (d) (i) *one of:* fertiliser; replaces nutrients; not enough nitrogen in the soil   1
          one of: increases yield; better crops; synthesis of proteins   1
       (ii) gets into rivers / eutrophication; contaminates drinking water   2

TOPIC 14 – Rates of reaction   (pages 66–67)

Homework questions

1 (a), (c), (f) [1 mark for 2 correct; 2 marks for all correct]   2

2 (a) at the start / where a tangent drawn to the curve is steepest   1
    (b) when the curve becomes flat (horizontal) / when a tangent drawn to the curve is horizontal   1

3 **B, D, A, C**   1

4 it reduces the distance between particles, making collisions more frequent   1

5 **C**   1

6 (a) iron
    (b) vanadium(V) oxide
    (c) nickel   3

Examination question

(a) (i) temperature (of acid) – allow time   1
     (ii) volume (of carbon dioxide)   1
     (iii) mass of calcium carbonate / volume of acid / concentration of acid   1
(b) *two from:* increase the concentration; increase the surface area **or** grind up   2

(c) **1**   1
     steeper curve   1
(d) (i) faster after 1 minute / slower after 2 minutes   1
     (ii) reactants get used up   1
         so concentration decreases / less chance of collisions   1

TOPIC 15 – More about reactions (pages 70–71)

Homework questions

1 Exothermic means heat energy is released during the reaction. Endothermic means heat energy is taken in during the reaction.   2

2 exothermic   1

3 equilibrium moves to the left   1

4 equilibrium moves to the right   1

5 equilibrium moves to the right   1

6 (a) equilibrium moves to the left   1
    (b) equilibrium moves to the right   1
    (c) equilibrium moves to the right   1

7 A higher temperature would increase the rate of the reaction. However, because this reaction is exothermic in the forward direction, a temperature increase favours the reverse, endothermic reaction, so less ammonia would be made.   1

8 catalysts speed up the rate at which equilibrium is reached, but do not affect the equilibrium position   1

Examination questions

1 (a) breaking C—H (carbon–hydrogen)   1
       breaking O=O (oxygen–oxygen)   1
       making C=O (carbon–oxygen)   1
       making O—H (oxygen–hydrogen)   1
    (b) x – energy needed to break bonds   1
       has to be supplied / activation energy   1
       y – energy released when bonds form   1
       so because y is greater in magnitude than x 1
       the overall reaction is exothermic   1

2 (a) 16%   1
    (b) iron is a catalyst   1
       which speeds up the reaction   1
    (c) *any 8 from:*
       best yield at high pressures; and low temperatures; reversible reaction; formation of ammonia is favoured by low temperatures; because reaction is exothermic; formation of ammonia is favoured by high pressure; greater number of reactant molecules than product molecules; pressure limited by cost of plant / safety; rate slow at low temperatures; actual temperature and pressure is a compromise; removal of ammonia makes rate more important than yield   8

113

Examination answers

TOPIC 16 – Electrolysis   (pages 74–75)

Homework questions

1 (c), (e), (g) [1 mark for 2 correct]   2

2 anode (positive electrode)   1

3 (a) bromine   (b) lead   2

4 (a) Na^+, Cl^-, H^+, OH^- 1
   (b) hydrogen at cathode ($-$) and chlorine at anode ($+$)   1
   (c) Sodium and hydrogen ions are both positive ions so go to cathode. Hydrogen is lower in activity so is discharged at the cathode. Chlorine is discharged in preference to oxygen at the anode. 3
   (d) products would be *sodium* and chlorine   1

5 (a) **B** and **D**   2
   (b) they contain ions that can move around and carry charge   1

6 (a) K   (b) $-2e^-$ (c) $+2e^-$ (d) O_2 4

7 anode ($+$): $Cu - 2e^- \longrightarrow Cu^{2+}$ 1
  cathode ($-$): $Cu^{2+} + 2e^- \longrightarrow Cu$ 1

Examination questions

1 (a) (i) **A**   (ii) **B**   (iii) **D**   3
   (b) $CuSO_4$ 1

2 (a) **A** = chlorine; **B** = hydrogen   1
   (b) moist universal indicator paper / litmus paper   1
     is bleached   1
   (c) (i) $2H^+ + 2e^- \longrightarrow H_2$ 1
     (ii) reduction   1
     (iii) *two from:* ammonia / hydrochloric acid / margarine / methanol   2
   (d) sodium hydroxide   1

TOPIC 17 – Acids, alkalis and salts
                             (pages 78–79)

Homework questions

1 alkalis are soluble in water, bases are not   1
  E.g. alkali – sodium hydroxide; base – copper oxide   2

2 (a) vinegar   1

3 sting is alkaline   1

4 (a) $KNO_3 + H_2O$ 1
   (b) $Na_2CO_3 + 2HCl$ 1

5 H^+ and OH^- 2

6 (a) potassium sulfate   1
   (b) copper(II) nitrate   1

7 (a) sodium hydroxide is soluble in water, copper hydroxide is not   1
   (b) when neutralising an acid with an alkali   1
   (c) when preparing an insoluble salt   1
   (d) to concentrate the solution and start the formation of crystals   1

Examination questions

1 (a) sulfuric   1
   (b) exothermic   1
   (c) Na_2SO_4 1
   (d) (i) hydrogen   1
     (ii) a lighted splint burns with a pop   1
     (iii) zinc chloride   1

2 (a) $H^+ (aq) + OH^- (aq) \longrightarrow H_2O (l)$ 1
   (b) nitric acid and ammonia   2

3 (a) (i) lead chloride is insoluble in water   1
     (ii) $PbCl_2$ (s)   2
   (b) (i) copper hydroxide / $Cu(OH)_2$
     (ii) lead sulfate / $PbSO_4$
     (iii) no precipitate [1 mark each]   5

TOPIC 18 – The Periodic Table   (pages 84–85)

Homework questions

1 (a) John Newlands   1
   (b) Dmitri Mendeleev   1

2 atomic numbers (and possibly mass numbers – depending on which version of the table is looked at) 1

3 transition metals   1

4 all have 1 electron in outer shell (highest energy level) 1

5 all have 7 electrons in outer shell (highest energy level)   1

6 (a) caesium (or francium – depending on which version of the table is looked at   1
   (b) fluorine   1

7 they react with water to make alkaline solutions   1

8 **D**   1

9 (a) I^- 1
   (b) ionic   1
   (c) sodium chloride and bromine   1

10 they form coloured compounds   1

Examination questions

1 **1** – an alkali metal; **2** – a transition metal used in the form of steel; **3** – a transition metal that weathers to a green colour; **4** – a noble gas   4

2 (a) atomic number   1
   (b) (i) sodium or potassium   1
     (ii) silicon / phosphorus / sulfur / chlorine   1
   (c) (i) 7 electrons in outer shell   1
     (ii) same atomic number / number of protons   1
       different mass number / number of neutrons   1
     (iii) outer shell is closer to the nucleus to attract an extra electron   1
       attractive force on incoming electron is greater because there are fewer shells   1

Examination answers

TOPIC 19 – More about acids and bases
(pages 88–89)

Homework questions

1 (a) $H^+ + NO_3^-$ 2
   (b) $2H^+ + SO_4^{2-}$ 2

2 strong – hydrochloric, sulfuric, nitric   3
   weak – carbonic, ethanoic, citric, tartaric   4

3 H^+ ions (protons) are produced when an acid is
   added to water. These react with hydroxide ions
   (OH^-) during neutralisation.   1

4 **C** nitric acid   1

5 **C**, the others are almost completely dissociated
   (ionised)   1

6 **A** Priestley   1

7 burettes deliver very accurate volumes of liquid to
   the reaction container   1

8 (a) $KNO_3 + H_2O$ 1
   (b) $CH_3COONa + H_2O$ 1

9 0.16 mol/dm^3 1

10 phenolphthalein   1

Examination questions

1 (a) sodium ions / chloride ions (sodium chloride
        solution)   1
   (b) $H^+ + OH^- \longrightarrow H_2O$ 1
        H^+ comes from dilute hydrochloric acid   1
        OH^- comes from sodium hydroxide solution   1

2 (a) $OH^- + H^+ \longrightarrow H_2O$ 2
        [1 mark for reactants, 1 mark for products]
   (b) (i)   27.5°C   1
        (ii) neutralisation complete at highest
              temperature   1
              according to the balanced equation, sodium
              hydroxide and hydrochloric acid react 1 : 1
              (1 mole reacts with 1 mole)   1
              but we need a greater volume of acid than
              alkali so the alkali must be more concentrated 1
   (c) 40 g   1
        $\frac{100}{40}$ 1
        2.5 mol/dm^3 1

TOPIC 20 – Aqueous chemistry   (pages 92–93)

Homework questions

1 (a) a solid which can dissolve in a liquid   1
   (b) a liquid which can dissolve a solid   1
   (c) a mixture of a solute and solvent   1

2 evaporates; cools; rain; absorbed; transpiration   5

3 (a) it forms a scum when shaken with soap solution   1
   (b) Ca^{2+} and Mg^{2+} 2

   (c) *3 advantages from:* tastes better; good for teeth
        and bones; reduces heart problems; better for
        brewing   3
        3 disadvantages from: forms scum not lather;
        wastes soap; wastes energy by forming fur inside
        kettles, boilers, etc.; can completely block hot-
        water pipes and boilers   3

4 Hot water used as an industrial coolant can get into
   rivers and lakes so causing thermal pollution.   1
   Reduces oxygen content in water so animals become
   distressed or even die.   1

5 *Sedimentation* – insoluble solids settle out at bottom
   of container   1
   Filtration – removal of smaller solids present in tap
   water   1
   Chlorination – water treatment using chlorine to kill
   bacteria and make water safe to drink   1

6 crystals forming   1

7 in areas where fresh water is scarce, e.g. Middle East,
   central America, Africa, etc.   1

8 sodium chloride   1

Examination questions

1 (a) calcium and magnesium   2
   (b) (i)   calcium / magnesium ions removed from
              solution so water softened   1
        (ii) lather   1

2 (a) to remove solids   1
   (b) to kill bacteria   1
   (c) **A** – 2, **B** – 3, **C** – 1   2
        (one mark for one pair correct)

3 (a) 100 g   1
   (b) solubility increases   1
        as temperature rises   1
        solubility of NaCl hardly changes   1
        potassium nitrate is a lot more soluble at higher
        temperatures   1
        solubility of both at 12–14°C is 25 g   [5 max.] 1

TOPIC 21 – Energy   (pages 96–97)

Homework questions

1 all except (a)   1

2 copper is a much better thermal energy conductor
   than glass   1

3 (a) $100 \times 4.2 \times 20 = 8400 \text{ J or } 8.4 \text{ kJ}$
        [1 for calculation; 1 for answer; 1 for unit]   3
   (b) $8.4 / 0.4 = 21 \text{ kJ per gram of ethanol}$
        [1 for calculation; 1 for answer; 1 for unit]   3
   (c) $C_2H_5OH + 3O_2 \longrightarrow 2CO_2 + 3H_2O$ 4

4 $(20 + 18) \times 4.2 \times (24 - 16) = 38 \times 4.2 \times 8$
   $= 1276.8 \text{ J}$ 4

Examination answers

5 (a) $10 \times 4.2 \times 6 = 252$ J   3
   (b) exothermic   1
   (c) correct diagram showing ΔH as negative   1

6 correct diagram showing ΔH as positive   1

Examination question

(a) (i) $4(O-H) = 4 \times 464 = 1856$ kJ   1
      $2(O-O) = 2 \times 146 = 292$ kJ   1
   (ii) $4(O-H) = 4 \times 464 = 1856$ kJ   1
      $1(O=O) = 498$ kJ   1
   (iii) $+2148 - 2354 = -206$ kJ (allow 206 kJ)   1
   (iv) exothermic; ΔH is negative (more heat given out than is taken in)   1
(b) (i) minimum energy required for reaction to take place   1
   (ii) **B**   1
   (iii) lowers the activation energy   1

TOPIC 22 – Detection and identification

(pages 100–101)

Homework questions

1 sodium carbonate (or sodium hydrogencarbonate)   1

2 ammonia   1

3 zinc carbonate   1

4 iron(III) nitrate   1

5 $CuCO_3 \longrightarrow CuO + CO_2$ 2

6 a cream coloured precipitate forming   1

7 potassium, K^+ ion   1

8 $CuSO_4 \text{ (aq)} + BaCl_2 \text{ (aq)} \longrightarrow BaSO_4 \text{ (s)} + CuCl_2 \text{ (aq)}$ 2

9 Dissolve both solids in separate test-tubes with dilute nitric acid followed by silver nitrate solution. Sodium chloride would give a white precipitate; sodium iodide would form a pale yellow precipitate.   1

10 Carry out a flame test. Barium gives an apple green flame.   1

11 Dissolve in water, and add sodium hydroxide solution. Both would form white precipitates. If excess sodium hydroxide solution is added, the precipitate from aluminium chloride would dissolve. There would be no change with excess sodium hydroxide solution if the original solid was magnesium chloride.   1

Examination questions

1 (a) **A** iron(III) chloride   1
   (b) **B** iron(II) chloride   1
   (c) **C** hydrogen   1
   (d) **D** iron(III) hydroxide   1
   (e) **E** silver chloride   1

2 (a) yellow   1
   (b) (i) zinc carbonate   1
      (ii) copper bromide   1
      (iii) magnesium sulfate   1
      (iv) copper bromide   1
      (v) zinc carbonate   1
   (c) white precipitate / solid   1

TOPIC 23 – Analysis

(pages 104–105)

Homework questions

1 carbon dioxide and water   2

2 (a) $CO_2 + 2H_2O$ 2
   (b) $C_3H_8 + 5O_2$ 2
   (c) $8O_2, 6H_2O$ 2

3 (a) 1.96 g   1
   (b) 0.84 g   1

4 (a) C_2H_4O 1
   (b) $C_4H_8O_2$ 1

5 well-written paragraph on each technique   6

Examination questions

1 (a) they will both produce: carbon dioxide and water   1
   (b) **A** has a trough at O—H absorption but **B** does not, showing the O—H group is not present   1

2 (a) *any one of:* infra-red spectroscopy; UV spectroscopy; mass spectrometry; gas–liquid chromatography; nuclear magnetic resonance   1
   (b) *any two of:* electronics; computers; fibre optics linked to some idea of how it has helped *e.g.* speed / sensitivity / accuracy / only need small samples   1

Data Sheet

1   Reactivity Series of Metals

Potassium	most reactive
Sodium	
Calcium	
Magnesium	
Aluminium	
Carbon	
Zinc	
Iron	
Tin	
Lead	
Hydrogen	
Copper	
Silver	
Gold	
Platinum	least reactive

(elements in italics, though non-metals, have been included for comparison).

---

2   Formulae of Some Common Ions

Positive ions

Name	Formula
Hydrogen	H^+
Sodium	Na^+
Silver	Ag^+
Potassium	K^+
Lithium	Li^+
Ammonium	NH_4^+
Barium	Ba^{2+}
Calcium	Ca^{2+}
Copper(II)	Cu^{2+}
Magnesium	Mg^{2+}
Zinc	Zn^{2+}
Lead	Pb^{2+}
Iron(II)	Fe^{2+}
Iron(III)	Fe^{3+}
Aluminium	Al^{3+}

Negative ions

Name	Formula
Chloride	Cl^-
Bromide	Br^-
Fluoride	F^-
Iodide	I^-
Hydroxide	OH^-
Nitrate	NO_3^-
Oxide	O^{2-}
Sulfide	S^{2-}
Sulfate	SO_4^{2-}
Carbonate	CO_3^{2-}

3 The Periodic Table of Elements

1	2											3	4	5	6	7	0
7 **Li** Lithium 3	9 **Be** Beryllium 4											11 **B** Boron 5	12 **C** Carbon 6	14 **N** Nitrogen 7	16 **O** Oxygen 8	19 **F** Fluorine 9	4 **He** Helium 2
23 **Na** Sodium 11	24 **Mg** Magnesium 12											27 **Al** Aluminium 13	28 **Si** Silicon 14	31 **P** Phosphorus 15	32 **S** Sulfur 16	35.5 **Cl** Chlorine 17	20 **Ne** Neon 10
39 **K** Potassium 19	40 **Ca** Calcium 20	45 **Sc** Scandium 21	48 **Ti** Titanium 22	51 **V** Vanadium 23	52 **Cr** Chromium 24	55 **Mn** Manganese 25	56 **Fe** Iron 26	59 **Co** Cobalt 27	59 **Ni** Nickel 28	64 **Cu** Copper 29	65 **Zn** Zinc 30	70 **Ga** Gallium 31	73 **Ge** Germanium 32	75 **As** Arsenic 33	79 **Se** Selenium 34	80 **Br** Bromine 35	40 **Ar** Argon 18
85 **Rb** Rubidium 37	88 **Sr** Strontium 38	89 **Y** Yttrium 39	91 **Zr** Zirconium 40	93 **Nb** Niobium 41	96 **Mo** Molybdenum 42	99 **Tc** Technetium 43	101 **Ru** Ruthenium 44	103 **Rh** Rhodium 45	106 **Pd** Palladium 46	108 **Ag** Silver 47	112 **Cd** Cadmium 48	115 **In** Indium 49	119 **Sn** Tin 50	122 **Sb** Antimony 51	128 **Te** Tellurium 52	127 **I** Iodine 53	84 **Kr** Krypton 36
133 **Cs** Caesium 55	137 **Ba** Barium 56	139 **La** Lanthanum 57	178 **Hf** Hafnium 72	181 **Ta** Tantalum 73	184 **W** Tungsten 74	186 **Re** Rhenium 75	190 **Os** Osmium 76	192 **Ir** Iridium 77	195 **Pt** Platinum 78	197 **Au** Gold 79	201 **Hg** Mercury 80	204 **Tl** Thallium 81	207 **Pb** Lead 82	209 **Bi** Bismuth 83	**Po** Polonium 84	**At** Astatine 85	131 **Xe** Xenon 54
Fr Francium 87	226 **Ra** Radium 88	227 **Ac** Actinium 89															**Rn** Radon 86

Elements 58-71 and 90-103 have been omitted.

Index

Published in 2006 by:
Nelson Thornes Ltd
Delta Place
27 Bath Road
CHELTENHAM
GL53 7TH
United Kingdom

06 07 08 09 10 / 10 9 8 7 6 5 4 3 2 1

A catalogue record for this book is available from the British Library

ISBN 0 7487 8376 8

Page make-up by Tech-set Ltd.

Printed in Croatia by Zrinski

Acknowledgements
We would like to thank examiners John Donneky and David Horrocks for their help with the examination questions, answers and tips.

AQA examination questions are reproduced by permission of the Assessment and Qualifications Alliance. AQA take no responsibility for answers given to their questions within this publication.

Photograph acknowledgements
Martyn Chillmaid, pp.35T, 79, 101TL, TR, M, B; A Davies, p.25B; A Sieneking, p.25T.

Every effort has been made to trace al the copyright holders, but if any have been overlooked, the publisher will be pleased to make the necessary arrangements at the first opportunity.